FOWKE, Bob

Victorians

Who? What? When?

Victorians

TOOT!

By Bob Fowke
With drawings by Andrew Mee

Hodder
Children's
Books

a division of Hodder Headline Limited

Plea for forgiveness

On 20 June 1837, Victoria's uncle William IV died and young Victoria became Queen of Great Britain. She was short, she was plump and she was just eighteen. When she died in 1901 having reigned for sixty-four years, she was still short but she was nearly eighty-two. She'd gone from plump to fat and was as wide as she was tall. And while she'd grown fatter, Britain had grown more powerful. Britain had become a world super power, as America is today.

So much happened during the adventure which was Victorian Britain, so many people did so many amazing things, that it's impossible to include more than a fraction of it all even in a shelf-full of books. This book takes the most important bits, the bits you need to know about for your studies or simply if you want to grasp the basics of this extraordinary period. Pity the poor author who had to decide what those important bits are, and forgive him if he's left out anything which you think should be in.

Bob Fowke

disasters

school

movements

royals

philanthropists

How to read this book

wars and rebellions

Entries are listed alphabetically. If you prefer to, you can find which page someone or something is on by looking in the index starting on page 123.

home life

doctors and nurses

empires

scientists and thinkers

Words followed by* - you can look up what they mean in the glossary starting on page 121.

sport and recreation

Names in **bold** in the text are of people who have their own entry. The little number in the margin beside them shows which page you'll find them on.

politicians

workers

transport

On the next page, there's a time chart showing how major people and events were connected.

soldiers

writers and artists

explorers

criminals

inventors, engineers and manufacturers

stamps

When?

1832	First Reform Act abolishes 'rotten' boroughs and gives the vote to most middle class men.
1833	Factory Act limits the working hours of children.
1833	Slavery ended in the British Empire.
1834	Tolpuddle Martyrs sentenced to deportation, having tried to form a Trades Union.
1837	Victoria becomes Queen.
1838	People's Charter demands more reforms of Parliament.
1839-41	First Opium War with China.
1839-42	First Afghan War.
1840	Victoria marries Prince Albert.
1842	Mines Act bans women and children from working underground.
1844	Factory Act further limits the working hours of children and also of women.
1845-9	Irish Potato Famine.
1846	Corn Laws repealed, allowing grain to be imported.
1847	Ten Hours Act further reduces working hours of women and children.
1851	Great Exhibition.
1854-6	Crimean War fought against the Russians.
1857-8	Second Opium War against the Chinese.
1861	Prince Albert dies.
1868	Disraeli and Gladstone become Prime Ministers for the first time (one after the other of course).

1870	Married Women's Property Act allows married women control of their own property.
1871	Trades Unions made legal.
1877	Victoria given the title 'Empress of India'.
1878-81	Second Afghan War.
1879	Zulu War
1884	Third Reform Bill increases the number of voters to five million.
1885	General Gordon killed at Khartoum by troops of the rebel leader 'The Mahdi'.
1886	Home Rule Bill defeated so no Home Rule for Ireland.
1887	Victoria's Golden Jubilee.
1893	Independent Labour Party formed by Keir Hardy.
1897	Victoria's Diamond Jubilee.
1897	Battle of Omdurman, Kitchener defeats rebel Sudanese forces.
1899-1901	Boer War.
1901	Victoria dies.

⚔ Afghan Wars

where wild tribesmen wandered ...

1839-42 & 1878-81

In Victorian newspaper cartoons Russia was often drawn as a bear - a big, grumpy bear. The nightmare for the British was that this Russian bear would invade southwards across the Northwest Frontier and take India away from them. Afghanistan, a wild mountainous region was the gateway through which the bear would have to come. So both Britain and Russia needed a friendly government in Kabul, the Afghan capital, and usually, what was friendly for one was unfriendly for the other.

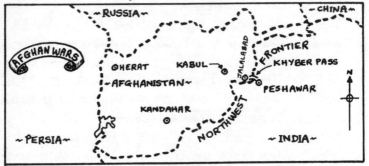

The British invaded Afghanistan three times in order to keep the Russians out, but British control was always limited. Worst of all, on 6 January 1842, a British army of 4,500 together with 12,000 followers was forced to leave Kabul. During their long retreat to India, they were harassed all the way by wild tribesmen. It was a bloodbath.

After the British took Kabul in 1881, the boundaries of modern Afghanistan were agreed between the British and the Russians.

👑 Albert, Prince Consort
hard-working German husband
1819-61

111 Albert, a German prince, and **Queen Victoria**, a young British Queen, were first cousins. It's always difficult for royalty to find suitably royal people to marry, so they married each other and it was a blissfully happy marriage. They had nine children and eventually there were thirty-seven grandchildren.

Albert was clever and handsome and honest. But he was also foreign and the British upper classes never really forgave him for that. He was only ever allowed to be 'Prince Consort' – the husband of the Queen, and he was never allowed any other title or any real power. Fortunately Victoria adored him so it didn't matter too much. Albert worked hard for the abolition of evils such as the slave trade and to improve British science and the British arts. He was a good musician.

Sadly Prince Albert died of typhoid fever when he was only forty-two. From that day on, Victoria never made any important decisions without first asking herself 'what Albert would have done'. His greatest memorial is the complex of museums and other buildings in South Kensington, including the Science Museum, the Royal Albert Hall and the Albert Memorial opposite them in Hyde Park in London.

Anderson, Elizabeth Garrett
doctor with a difference

1836-1917

Elizabeth Garrett Anderson was the first properly qualified woman doctor in Britain. She had to study privately under friendly male doctors because no medical school of the time would let her in - because she was a woman. Despite the difficulties, in 1865 she was licensed to practise medicine by the Society of Apothecaries (they changed their rules afterwards to stop women applying in future). A year later she founded the St. Mary's Dispensary in London which later grew into the famous Elizabeth Garrett Anderson Hospital for women. Throughout her life Elizabeth supported women's struggle for the right to vote. In 1908 she was elected Mayor of Aldeburgh, thus becoming the first woman mayor in Britain as well as the first woman doctor.

Anti-Corn Law League *see* **Corn Laws**

Arnold, Thomas
headmaster who helped sport

1795-1842

Thomas Arnold became headmaster of Rugby School in 1828. At that time British public **schools** were rough, tough places. There had been riots at

91

Winchester when the local soldiers had to be called in to keep order. There had even been a riot at Rugby. Arnold was firm but fair. He expelled troublemakers and encouraged prefects to keep order. He also modernised what was taught. For the first time, pupils could learn maths, modern history and modern languages, and not just ancient Greek and Latin and ancient history. Arnold also encouraged sport which he saw as an important part of the school's activities. Rugby school was where rugby football was invented.

People noticed that ex-Rugby boys tended to be serious, honest and hard-working - just the sort of men who were needed to run the **British Empire**. Other schools began to copy Arnold's example and soon British public schools were no longer quite the rough, tough places they used to be.

Barnardo, Thomas John
founder of homes
1845-1905

Thomas Barnardo was a serious young man and a keen Christian. Aged twenty-one, he moved to London to study medicine because he wanted to be a missionary to China. But once in London he saw how many desperately poor, unwanted children there were on the city's streets and he was horrified. He began to work part time for a 'ragged school' for the poor, and in 1870 he opened a home for 'destitute boys' in Stepney in East London – and gave up any idea of going to China.

When he died there were over ninety 'Dr. Barnardo's homes' all over Britain and Canada (where he sent many children for training and to settle). No child who needed protection was ever turned away from his doors. He rescued a total of 59,384 children from dreadful poverty. The movement he started continues to this day.

Beeton, Mrs Isabella Mary

 housekeeping expert and
first ever celebrity chef
1836-65

Isabella Beeton was the eldest daughter in a family of twenty-one children. She and the others were brought up by their grandmother, in part of the grandstand at Epsom racecourse of all places. She helped her grandmother and became a very skilful cook and housekeeper.

In 1856 Isabella married Sam Beeton, an up-and-coming publisher. Sam had already started a women's magazine, the *English Woman's Domestic Magazine* (1852). Isabella became a vital part of the family publishing business, both as an editor and as a writer. She's most famous for her *Book of Household Management*. It contains a wealth of easy-to-follow recipes and tips on running a Victorian home and it was very popular with the new Victorian middle class, the sort of people who perhaps had one

⁹² **servant** but where the mistress also cooked and helped with the housework. Isabella died when she was only twenty-eight. Sam was heartbroken. He'd lost a brilliant business partner as well as a wife.

Bell, Alexander Graham

Scotsman who invented the telephone

1847-1922

Alexander Graham Bell invented the telephone. The invention grew out of his interest in making electrical hearing aids for deaf people. The idea of converting speech into an electrical signal which could travel down a wire and be reconverted back into sound came to him in 1865 while he was engaged on this work. Soon after, he emigrated from Scotland, first to Canada and then to the USA. It was there that he put his idea into practice (1870). The first words ever spoken successfully down a telephone line were to his assistant Watson: 'Mr Watson, come here. I want you' - Bell had spilt battery acid on his trousers!

Bell went on to found the Bell Telephone Corporation and became extremely rich, but he never lost his interest in helping deaf people. He married a woman who had been very deaf from childhood. He even published a book, *Upon a Formation of a Deaf Variety of the Human Race* (1884), which is about the understandable tendency of some deaf people to marry other deaf people and to have deaf children. He also invented a hydrofoil boat which could reach speeds of 112 kph (70 mph), an improved gramophone, flat disc records, a forerunner of the iron lung, a method for removing salt from sea water and a kite which could carry a man high above the ground.

⚔ Boer War
scorched earth in South Africa
1899-1902

In the nineteenth century two groups of Europeans vied for control of southern Africa: the British and the Boers. The Boers were the descendants of Dutch colonists who founded the Cape Colony back in 1652. By 1815 the British were in control. The Boers disliked British rule. Many of them trekked north from the Cape Colony (1835-43) to found two new Boer states, the Orange Free State and the Transvaal.

There were diamonds and gold in the Boer states and most of the mine owners were British. Yet again the Boers felt threatened. In 1899, led by President Kruger of the Transvaal, they besieged the British cities of Mafeking, Ladysmith and Kimberley.

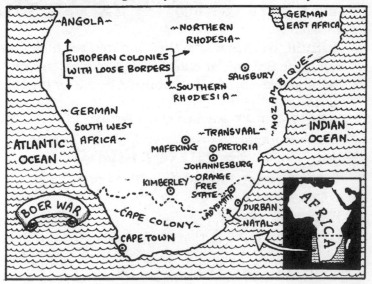

In reality the Boers had done a very stupid thing, because Britain was so much more powerful. Under their commander General Kitchener, the British shipped in reinforcements. Soon 500,000 British troops faced just 80,000 Boers. The besieged towns were relieved and Kruger left for Europe. However, Boer soldiers fought on. Kitchener decided that a 'scorched earth' policy was the only way to force them to surrender: Boer farms (and African farms - Africans tended to support the British against the Boers but the British let them down in this and other ways) were destroyed and Boer men, women and children were rounded up into 'concentration camps'. These weren't death camps like the Nazi concentration camps, but they were appalling all the same. Over 20,000 died due to the poor conditions.

In 1910, Transvaal and the Orange Free State joined with the British Cape and Natal colonies to form the 'Union of South Africa'- South Africa as it is now.

Booth, William *see* **Salvation Army**

✗ Boxer Rising
Chinese who fought foreigners
1898-1900

Members of the 'Society of Righteous and Harmonious Fists', *I-ho Chüan* in Chinese, or 'Boxers' in English, believed that their strange boxing exercises protected them from harm by bullets and other weapons. The Boxers were mainly poor peasants but there were retired members of the Chinese Imperial Guard among them.

China in the 1890s was a mess. To patriotic Chinese it seemed that the country was being carved up by greedy and powerful foreigners: British, French, German, Russian and Japanese. Starting in 1898, bands of Boxers roamed north China killing Chinese converts to Christianity, a foreign religion, and destroying all things foreign, especially churches and railways.

In June 1900, the old dowager Empress Tz'u-hsi gave the green light to Boxer attacks on foreigners in Peking. All foreign legations in the city were besieged, and the foreigners inside were in danger of being massacred. An international relief force of 19,000 men was quickly cobbled together on the coast and marched inland to the rescue. This force took Peking on 14 August and looted it. In September 1901 a final settlement was agreed with the Chinese court. The Chinese had to pay over a huge sum of money to get the foreign force to leave.

 British Empire
it got burdensomely big

From small beginnings in the early seventeenth century, the British Empire grew and grew, squeezing the rival French Empire into second place. Even the loss of all British North American colonies (except Canada) in 1783, didn't stop the growth. Not that the British government ever planned to have an empire. It just sort of *happened*. New colonies developed from the efforts of private settlers or private merchant companies, or as the result of wars which seemed defensive when they started, but nearly always ended up making the Empire bigger still.

The Empire was a muddle of different cultures and forms of government. Countries with large populations of British settlers, such as Australia, Canada and South Africa were mainly left to run their own affairs. Other countries were directly administered by their governors. Yet others were 'protectorates', countries such as Egypt which were officially independent but weren't really, or

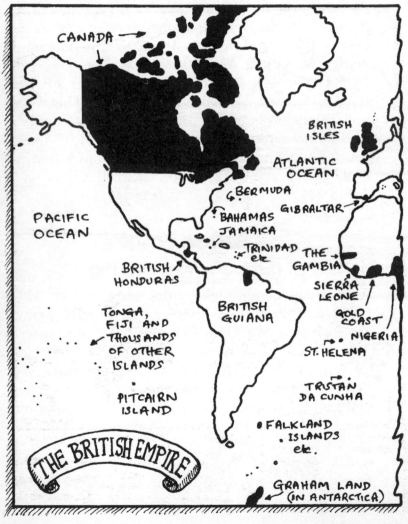

THE BRITISH EMPIRE

they were 'dependencies' which amounted to much the same thing. The whole show was run from the Colonial Office in London, set up in 1801. From there, governors were sent forth to govern, district officers were appointed to administer remote districts and the whole unwieldy mass was pushed and prodded as was deemed necessary by the British government.

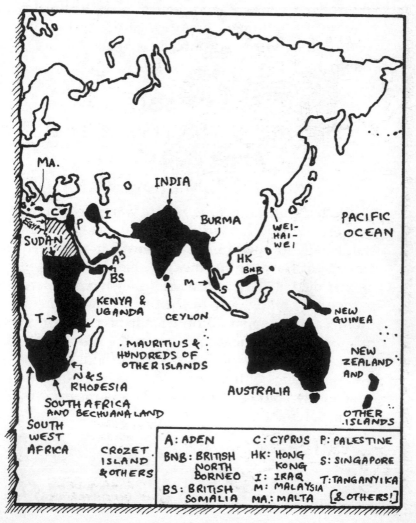

A: ADEN	C: CYPRUS	P: PALESTINE
BNB: BRITISH NORTH BORNEO	HK: HONG KONG	S: SINGAPORE
BS: BRITISH SOMALIA	I: IRAQ M: MALAYSIA MA: MALTA	T: TANGANYIKA [& OTHERS!]

India was the largest and richest of all the countries in the Empire, the 'Jewel in the Crown' as it's been called. Until the 'Indian Mutiny' of 1857-9 it was ruled by the East India Company. After that it was run directly by the British government under a 'Viceroy' appointed from Britain. Meanwhile the British started to boast of their duty to 'pick up the white man's burden' and to rule 'less fortunate' races. In the 'scramble for Africa' at the end of the century, the British scrambled as much as other countries.

Brontë sisters
Charlotte 1816-55, Emily 1818-48, Anne 1820-49
young Yorkshire novelists

Charlotte, Emily and Anne Brontë were three of the greatest Victorian writers. They spent their childhood with their brother Bramwell in the lonely vicarage of Haworth on the Yorkshire moors. Their mother died in 1821, a year after they moved there, so they were brought up by their father, the reverend Brontë, a strange man. Brontë made his children eat potatoes without meat to toughen them up. When upset, he shot pistols from the kitchen door or destroyed items of furniture. The children filled the long, lonely hours by writing endless stories and by walking on the moors.

ONCE UPON A TIME...

Their best known books are: *Jane Eyre* by Charlotte, *Wuthering Heights* by Emily and *The Tenant of Wildfell Hall* by Anne. Bramwell tried to be an artist but was not successful. He died in 1848 and Emily soon followed him, as did Anne. Charlotte married her father's curate, Mr Nicholls, and lived another seven years. After that, Mr Nicholls and the Reverend Brontë lived on alone in the vicarage.

✐ Brunel, Isambard Kingdom

energetic engineer of ships and railways

1806-59

Isambard Brunel was the son of Marc Brunel, the engineer who built the first tunnel under the Thames, in the 1820s. While working for his father, he once worked for ninety-six hours without a break.

Brunel is best known for his work on the Great Western Railway, especially for the Royal Albert Bridge across the Tamar near Plymouth, and for his ships.

Realising that large ships need less power than smaller ships in proportion to their weight (because their surface area is smaller in proportion to their total volume), he built huge iron ships which could carry fuel for longer journeys than their smaller rivals – and carry it faster. His massive *Great Western* crossed the Atlantic four days faster than the *Sirius* which was half its size. Later he built the *Great Britain*, now a museum in Bristol, the first large ship to be driven by screw propellers.

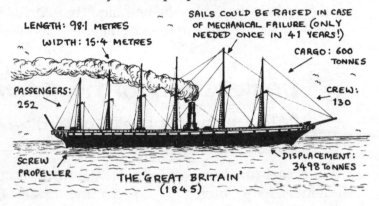

LENGTH: 98·1 METRES
WIDTH: 15·4 METRES
SAILS COULD BE RAISED IN CASE OF MECHANICAL FAILURE (ONLY NEEDED ONCE IN 41 YEARS!)
CARGO: 600 TONNES
PASSENGERS: 252
CREW: 130
SCREW PROPELLER
DISPLACEMENT: 3498 TONNES
THE 'GREAT BRITAIN' (1845)

Burton, Sir Richard Francis
vigorous voyager to various places
1821-90

Sir Richard Burton spent his childhood travelling from place to place round Europe like a rich gypsy. He learned to speak six languages and how to use a sword but he hardly ever went to school. Later, while in the army in India, he also learned Hindi, Gujerati, Sindhi, Punjabi, Farsi, Arabic, Sanskrit (written) and Camoen, which is spoken in Goa.

While in India, Burton studied eastern customs and culture, in particular Islamic culture. This helped him in his first major journey of exploration: to Mecca in Arabia which is forbidden to non-Muslims. Starting

in 1853, he travelled the whole way from London to Mecca in various disguises so that no one would get wind of his project. After his return, whenever he signed his name in Arabic, he called himself 'Al Haj (the Pilgrim) Abdullah'.

Burton's life is one long list of adventures, the most famous being a journey with John Hanning Speke to discover the source of the River Nile (1856-9). The book which made him the most money was his translation of *The Book of a Thousand Nights and a Night*, or *'Thousand and One Nights'*, first published 1885-6. He's buried at Mortlake in London, in a marble mausoleum carved to look like an Arab tent.

Cadbury, George
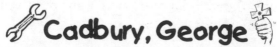

much more than a chocolate
1839-1922

Cadbury is not just a type of chocolate, it's a family name. George Cadbury and his brother Richard were

Quakers*. They were hard-working and honest. George never drank alcohol or smoked tobacco. When they took over the family cocoa business in 1861 George didn't take tea or coffee or read newspapers either.

The Cadburys always cared for their workers. They used to eat breakfast with them every morning – followed by a short religious service for those who wanted it. In 1879 the brothers moved their factory to the countryside at Bournville, then four miles south of Birmingham. George built a 'model village' of three hundred houses around the new factory for his workers to live in. The houses were light and comfortable with large gardens.

Richard died in 1899, but George kept going for many more years. His passion was adult education. Every Sunday until he was seventy-two, he would cycle into Birmingham to teach working men to read and write – and to give Bible classes.

Carroll, Lewis
(Charles Lutwidge Dodgson)
classic kids' writer and pioneer of photography

1832-98

Charles Dodgson was a funny, quiet man who taught mathematics at Oxford University. He was very shy and had a stammer. Perhaps because of this, he preferred the company of children to the company of adults. He's most famous for two children's books: *Alice's Adventures in Wonderland* and *Through the Looking Glass and What Alice Found There*. Alice in Wonderland came from stories told to Alice Liddell and her sisters (the daughters of the Dean of his Oxford college) during a boat trip one sunny afternoon in 1862.

Dodgson was also a pioneer of photography and took photographs of Alice among other subjects. His best serious work was *Euclid and his Modern Rivals* which shows why the ancient Greek mathematician Euclid was so brilliant. Unfortunately, many people refused to take his serious book seriously because there were so many jokes in it!

Chamberlain, Joseph
he brightened up Birmingham
1836-1914

Joseph Chamberlain made a fortune manufacturing screws in Birmingham. In 1874 when he was thirty-eight, he was so rich that he could retire. He threw himself into public works. As mayor of Birmingham (1873-5), he improved the city out of all recognition. By the time he'd finished, Birmingham had gas works for gas lighting, a sewage farm, the start of decent workers' housing and was on its way to a free library and art gallery.

In 1876 Chamberlain became a Liberal* member of Parliament and in 1889 he was made Secretary of State for the Colonies. He believed that the **British Empire** was good for the people ruled by it, and in 'Imperial Union' - that all the countries of the Empire should become a sort of super country. (Something the French tried to do with their empire.) Because of his support for the Empire he opposed **Gladstone's** plans for **Home Rule** for Ireland. He retired in 1906, dying eight years later – in Birmingham.

17

49

54

⚔ Charge of the Light Brigade
into the valley of death ...

1854

The Charge of the Light Brigade was when a jumper with buttons led a hopeless cavalry charge in defence of a woolly helmet – well it sounds like that. It happened on 25 October 1854 during the **Crimean War**. The Russian army was attacking the British supply port of Balaclava on the Black Sea. Lord Raglan, the British commander, noticed that the Russians had started to remove their guns from hills above the port. He gave orders for the Light Brigade to mount a cavalry attack.

37

Unfortunately, Raglan's orders were delayed. In the confusion, Lord Cardigan, the commander of the Light Brigade, took the order to mean that he should lead his force up a valley towards a very strong Russian artillery position and not along a hill which the Russians were withdrawing from. It was suicide to attack up that valley, but he did his duty - and so did the Light Brigade. They galloped straight at the Russian guns and 40% of them were killed. Cardigan himself galloped all the way there, right through the Russian lines, and all the way back. Then he went and had breakfast on his yacht. The mad exploit was celebrated by **Lord Alfred Tennyson** in his poem *The Charge of the Light Brigade*.

104

Lord Cardigan once issued his regiment of Light Hussars (lightly armed cavalry) with the 'cardigan jacket' – hence the word 'cardigan'. In the cold of the Crimean winter during the Battle of Balaclava, British soldiers often wore woolly helmets which covered their ears and chins as well as their heads – hence the word balaclava.

> ANY COMPLAINTS, LIEUTENANT?

> NO, SIR! WARM AS TOAST, SIR!

Chartists

people who petitioned Parliament

1838- *c.*1850

Chartism was a mass movement of working class people. It took its name from the 'People's Charter' published in 1838. There were six points to the charter. Five of them have happened and only one hasn't, so you could say that Chartism was successful. The six points were:

> *The vote for all adult men.*
> *Voting by secret ballots.*
> *No 'property qualification' for Members of Parliament – even poor men can be MPs.*
> *MPs to be paid (otherwise working men can't afford to spend time in Parliament).*
> *Each constituency which MPs represent to have roughly the same numbers of voters.*
> *Parliaments to be elected every year. (This is the one which hasn't happened.)*

Chartism was mainly peaceful, but there were a few

riots and rebellions. Chartist leaders were arrested, sent to prison or exiled to Australia. The Chartists went in for monster meetings of up to 200,000 people at a time and monster petitions to Parliament. The largest petition, in 1842, had three million signatures. The movement faded out in the 1850s and working men didn't start to get the vote until the late 1860s.

🔨 Child labour
under age wage slaves

Small children chained to carts deep underground, pulling coal from the coal face for fourteen hours a day like donkeys. Little chimney sweeps scrabbling in the dark for brutal masters. Orphans bought like slaves from workhouses by factory owners. Little apprentices in the mills, cleaning up beneath the machines and often injured by moving machinery. Children who at night had to sleep beneath the machines that they worked on all day. Brutal overseers who beat their children to make them work harder. It's enough to make your heart bleed.

It was enough to make Victorian hearts bleed too. Throughout the nineteenth century a series of acts of Parliament gradually improved the working conditions of children.

93 **Lord Shaftesbury's Factory Act** of 1833 ordered that no child under nine could be employed in a textile mill and children aged 9-11 must work no more than nine hours per day.
The 1842 Coal Mines Act ordered that no women, girls or boys under ten could work down the mines.

An act of 1842 improved things for child chimney sweeps - 'climbing boys' as they were called.

The 1847 Ten Hours Act ordered that no women or young people could work more than ten hours per day.

 By 1901, the minimum working age for children was twelve, and women and young people could only work between the hours of 6.00 am to 6.00 pm.

Each act of parliament was met by squeals of horror from the more selfish factory owners. Children were a vital part of the labour force, and the most profitable because they were paid so little. More than a third of the work force in most early textile mills were children. The better masters made sure that their child employees received a basic education and were well looked after – after all, they would need their skilled labour as adults later.

children

paradise for the few

Before the Victorian age, children tended to be seen as little adults. They wore grown-up clothing and were expected to act grown up as soon as possible. It was the immense wealth of Victorian Britain which allowed the upper and middle classes the luxury of childhood. More and more books and toys were produced specially for children. The magic world of the children's nursery at the top of the house, looked after by a kindly nurse, was celebrated as a paradise.

Unfortunately, this paradise was for the few. The little darlings who lived their magic life in the nursery lived in another universe and were few in comparison to the number of filthy urchins who toiled their lives away in the factories and mines or begged for bread on the streets. The terrible contrast between the warm, bright nursery of the rich and the poor child looking in through the window from the cold outside was described in pitiful detail by writers 40 such as **Charles Dickens**.

Chimney Sweeps Act *see* **child labour**

Christmas trees
a German brought them

The fashion for dragging young fir trees into the house and decorating them with candles took root in Britain in the nineteenth century. Before then the British had preferred a large, leafless 'yule log'. Christmas trees were a German custom. It was the German **Prince Albert** who set up the first royal Christmas trees in Windsor Castle in 1841, soon after he and **Victoria** were married. He decorated them with candles, candies, fruit and ginger bread. Small tables beneath the trees were heaped high with presents. The fashion spread like wildfire because everyone wanted to copy the young royal family.

clothes
crinolines and other inconveniences

Victorian clothes were uncomfortable by modern standards, especially women's clothes. There were no artificial fibres, no plastics, no zips, no elastic. Materials were often heavy and tough.

For most of the period, men wore high stiff collars. Over their trousers and waistcoats they wore waisted coats. This style was gradually replaced by the three-piece lounge suit, ancestor of the modern businessman's suit, which came in gradually from the 1850s. From the 1840s, men's clothes became darker and more serious. The serious look went with the bushy side whiskers and being manly and important. The whiskers were shaved off again after around 1880 but the dark colours stayed for many more years as did being manly and important.

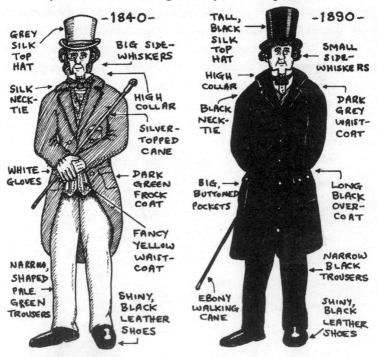

Women's clothes were bright and cheerful by comparison, but oh so uncomfortable. The crinoline came in in the 1850s, a construction of whalebone hoops which held the skirt wide from the body. It was so heavy that the crinoline cage, a steel framework, was invented in 1856 to replace it. In the

1860s, crinolines gave way to the rear bustle. But bustle or crinoline, all women's clothes needed huge swathes of material to give the right look. And all required the worst thing of all – a tight corset.

The fashionable look, especially late in the century demanded a 'wasp waist'. Most women don't have wasp waists – they're not wasps – so they laced themselves into shape. Corsets tied tight sometimes caused women to faint because they restricted breathing. They could even damage internal organs. In 1851 the American feminist Amelia Jenks Bloomer travelled to London to publicise her campaign for 'rational dress' for women, but her outfit, a jacket over baggy 'Turkish' trousers tied in at the ankle – 'bloomers' as they were known – never caught on. Women had to wait for World War I before getting into something more comfortable.

~1840~

SIMPLE HAT OR BONNET

COMPLEX HAIRSTYLE WITH RINGLETS

← LOW NECKLINE

LONG, FINE GLOVES

← NARROW WAIST

← CRINOLINE

FAN→

LONG, EMBROIDERED GOWN

~1890~

SWEPT-UP HAIR

NAVY BLUE TAILORED JACKET WITH PUFFED-UP SHOULDERS

VERY NARROW WAIST

CRINOLINE

LONG, NAVY BLUE SKIRT

FANCY HAT

HIGH COLLAR WITH TIE

WHITE WAIST-COAT

← WIDE CUFFS

← SHORT GLOVES

Conservative Party *see* **political parties**

Co-operative societies
shops which share

In an industrial co-operative, people work together for the common good, instead of being exploited by their employers. The idea of co-operatives was very appealing in the dark early days of the **Industrial Revolution**. A Welsh mill-owner called Robert Owen spoke and wrote widely about it. He tried to create an ideal industrial set-up in his own textile mills at New Lanark in Scotland.

56

~THE ORIGINAL CO-OP, ROCHDALE~

Industrial co-operatives never took off, but co-operative shops did. The first co-operative shop was opened in Rochdale in 1844 by a group of Owenites (followers of the ideas of Robert Owen) who called themselves the 'Rochdale Society of Equitable Pioneers'. It was a revolutionary concept - the customers were the owners of the store. Instead of profits from purchases going to shareholders they were given back to the customers as dividends, 'divvies' as they became known. The rules for the Rochdale store have set the standard for co-operatives from that day to this. Among them:

Membership open to everyone.
No political or religious discrimination.
The society to be controlled democratically by the members.

Co-operative shops spread like wildfire. By 1891 there were 1,300 stores with a total of over a million members. There are still a lot of them about.

Corn Laws
they kept out the competition
1846

If there's only one shop in town and only one tube of Smarties in that shop, chances are that someone will pay over the odds to get those Smarties – in other words, the less there is of something, the higher the price that traders can charge for it.

What goes for Smarties goes for barley, wheat, oats and rye. If you can keep out foreign imports so that there's less of them around, farmers will be able to charge a higher price. The Corn Laws were laws which limited the import of foreign cereals so that farmers and landowners could make more money.

The very earliest Corn Laws were passed in

the Middle Ages. At that time they were widely accepted because most people made their money from the land anyway. But by the nineteenth century, huge numbers of people worked in factories and never went anywhere near the land. The Corn Laws came to be seen as a way of protecting the interests of rich landowners against everyone else.

The 'Anti-Corn Law League' was founded in Manchester in 1839. Members campaigned long and hard. The break came in 1845, during the terrible 83 **Potato Famine** in Ireland when foreign food was desperately needed and the Corn Laws stopped food getting in to help the starving Irish. Prime 79 Minister **Robert Peel** repealed the Corn Laws in 1846. 48 This was seen as a victory for **Free Trade**.

⚔ Crimean War
reining in the Russians
1854-56

In the mid-nineteenth century, the Russian Empire 17 was expanding into Asia almost as fast as the **British Empire** was expanding everywhere else. The Russian Empire was one big lump of land, whereas the British Empire was scattered all over the place. The Russians began to threaten British communication with the British Empire in the east.

The Crimean War was fought between the British, French and Turks on one side and the Russians on the other side and its purpose was to stop Russian expansion to the south, and to stop the Russian navy causing trouble in the Black Sea. Most of the action took place around the Russian Black Sea port of Sevastopol in the Crimea. Both sides were very badly led and their soldiers suffered terribly. It was the scandalous hospital conditions of wounded British soldiers which led to reforms in health care by **Florence Nightingale**.

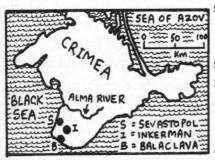

The Russians were defeated in three major battles: Alma River, Balaclava and Inkerman. Eventually they were forced to withdraw from Sevastopol.

Darwin, Charles Robert
he evolved a theory
1809-82

When Charles Darwin was a boy, most people thought that the Bible was literally true. God created the world around 4000 BC. He stuffed the Garden of Eden with all species of animals, and the species had stayed exactly the same from that time on.

Darwin was the son of a Shrewsbury doctor. His mother was a Unitarian* which meant that he was brought up to think for himself. In 1831 he joined a scientific expedition as ship's naturalist. The *HMS Beagle* sailed across the Atlantic and around South America to the Galapagos Islands in the Pacific. There Darwin noticed that the same species of birds, cut off for centuries on different islands, had developed in quite different ways so that they had almost become different species. This and other amazing discoveries led him to his theory of 'evolution by natural selection': that species 'evolve' over immense periods of time because only individuals which are best suited to their environments will survive and reproduce. Their offspring in turn tend to inherit and pass on whatever 'characteristics' helped the parents to survive. God had nothing to do with it, at least, not directly.

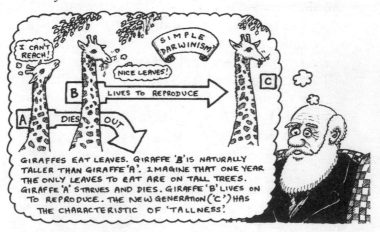

I CAN'T REACH!

SIMPLE DARWINISM

NICE LEAVES!

B

LIVES TO REPRODUCE

C

A

DIES OUT

GIRAFFES EAT LEAVES. GIRAFFE 'B' IS NATURALLY TALLER THAN GIRAFFE 'A'. IMAGINE THAT ONE YEAR THE ONLY LEAVES TO EAT ARE ON TALL TREES. GIRAFFE 'A' STARVES AND DIES. GIRAFFE 'B' LIVES ON TO REPRODUCE. THE NEW GENERATION ('C') HAS THE CHARACTERISTIC OF 'TALLNESS'.

Partly out of concern about Church reaction, Darwin didn't publish his ideas until 1858-9, long after the voyage was over. As predicted, *The Origin of Species by Means of Natural Selection* raised a storm of protest among Church leaders, but they were unable to rebut his arguments.

✎ Dickens, Charles
best-selling writer and adjective
1812-70

In early Victorian times, people could be sent to prison if they couldn't pay their debts. That's what happened to Charles Dickens's family in 1821, when he was just eleven years old. Charles was the only one of the family left on the outside. He found work in a warehouse and visited the prison on Sundays. Memories of that dreadful time never left him.

The family fortunes gradually improved. Charles became a journalist and learned to write. Success came with the publication of the *Pickwick Papers* (starting in 1836), a collection of funny stories in a monthly magazine. By the fifteenth month 40,000 copies were being sold and Dickens was on his way to becoming the most famous writer of the Victorian period. So famous that his name has become an adjective - the word 'Dickensian' is used to describe scenes of nineteenth-century gloom. Many of his books, such as *Oliver Twist*, describe the struggles of poor children against cruel and powerful adults.

Disraeli, Benjamin
Victoria's favourite Prime Minister
1804-81

49 Benjamin Disraeli and **William Gladstone** were like chalk and cheese. Disraeli was colourful and funny and a Tory*, Gladstone was serious and sober and a Liberal*. Between them they dominated Britain in 111 the last half of **Queen Victoria's** long reign. Victoria preferred Disraeli because he flattered her.

Disraeli entered Parliament in 1837. A clever speaker, he rose to fame in the 1840s by leading the Tory 79 attack on **Peel** over the repeal of the **Corn Laws**. 36 Later he reformed his party and in 1867 it was the Tories who introduced a Reform Bill. This greatly increased the number of men who were allowed to vote. Next year Disraeli became Prime Minister and his long duel with Gladstone began.

Even though he was twice Prime Minister, Disraeli was never your average British politician. Firstly, he was a Jew who converted to Christianity. Secondly, he was a talented writer. His first novel *Vivian Grey* was a big success, as were *Tancred*, *Coningsby* and *Sybil*. When he died, Victoria herself placed a wreath of flowers on his tomb.

WHEN I WANT TO READ A NOVEL, I WRITE ONE!

HO HO!

WHAT A WIT!

HEE HEE!

Dodgson, Charles *see* **Carroll, Lewis**

Eliot, George
good books - clever woman
1819-80

George Eliot is the pen name of Mary Anne (or Marian) Evans, later Mrs Cross, one of the great Victorian novelists. She first rose to fame with her novel *Adam Bede* (published 1859) which sold 16,000 copies within a year. Her greatest novels are: *Adam Bede*, *Middlemarch*, *The Mill on the Floss* and *Silas Marner*.

She and her partner George Henry Lewis (where the 'George' in George Eliot came from) were two of the ugliest people in London but they loved each other dearly. They lived together from 1854, but without marrying because he was already married. This was a shocking thing to do in those days. Many people would have nothing more to do with her. It was Lewis who encouraged 'George' to start writing novels.

Lewis died in 1878 and in 1880 Mary did finally get married - to a Mr Cross, a banker who was twenty years younger than her. But when her turn came to die, only seven months later, she was buried next to Lewis.

Factory acts
time to watch out for the workers

Why pass laws to protect poor workers from their rich employers? It's only the poor who benefit - and they're a menace. For most of history, it's been the rich who make the laws, laws which have tended to help the rich to stay rich.

BAH! I'M LOSING MONEY!

In the late eighteenth century, the attitudes of some wealthy lawmakers began to soften. It was difficult to ignore the suffering of workers in the new factories and mines. Difficult, and not very Christian. Most of the great Victorian reformers, such as **Lord** 93 **Shaftesbury**, were serious Christians.

The 'Health and Morals of Apprentices' act, controlling the treatment of poor apprentices, was 111 passed in 1802 long before **Victoria** came to the throne. It was the first law in modern times to interfere between master and worker on the side of the worker. Pressure for change grew stronger still in the 1830s due to a movement called the 'Short Time Movement' which called for shorter working hours. At last, in 1833, the 'Factory Act' was passed. It restricted child labour in the textile mills to just nine hours a day and ruled that factory children should have some minimum schooling. But the really big thing about the Factory Act was that it arranged for 'Factory Inspectors' to force owners to obey the new law. That was a major breakthrough.

Driven forward by Lord Shaftesbury, Parliament passed further 'factory acts' in the 1840s, including the Ten Hours Act of 1847, which limited the hours worked by women, children and young people.

Faraday, Michael
genius of the electric generator
1791-1867

Michael Faraday was almost completely self-taught, learning science while he worked as a bookbinder's apprentice. The kindly bookbinder let him read the books as well as bind them. In 1813, he became assistant to Humphry Davy, the most famous scientist of his day. Davy's wife treated Faraday like a servant but he ignored her rudeness and worked hard in the laboratory learning more all the time.

Faraday's greatest work was on electricity and magnetism. He worked out the principles of electrical induction: how electric current is produced within a magnetic field. Arising from this, he made the world's first electric generator. A copper wheel was mounted so that its rim passed between the poles of a magnet. When the wheel was turned, current flowed in the copper. All modern generators work on the same basic principle, although nowadays the wheels are massive.

Faraday was a systematic worker, as all great experimental scientists must be. He always numbered the paragraphs of his notes. The last was 3299. It represents a lifetime of invention.

 # food
meals for the masses

56
111
Before the **Industrial Revolution**, most people lived off the land. But by the time that **Victoria** came to the throne, millions of people lived in vast cities. Some never saw a cow or a pig from one year to the next. The food they ate was poor quality. Milk was watered down and then chalk and flour might be added to make it look right. It was normal to add lime, chalk and alum (for bleaching) to bread.

At the start of the century, there were no food factories and almost no processed foods. Things changed gradually. Due to greater availability of ice from Norway, fish became cheaper than meat and was widely eaten by working class families. In 1810 a method for sealing food into metal cans was patented* by Bryan Donkin at the Dartford Ironworks, following an earlier French invention using glass jars. In 1855 dried milk powder was invented and in the 1860s, margarine was developed by another Frenchman, Hyppolite Mège Mouriés. His invention was a mixture of emulsified* beef suet and milk, called 'margarinemouries' from his own name and *margaron* the Greek for a pearl. It tasted vile by modern standards but it was as near as many poor people came to butter.

Football Association
look, no hands!

1863

When football teams play each other it's important that both sides play by the same rules. At one time it was necessary to agree the rules before almost every match. The Football Association was formed in 1863 by several London clubs to develop a permanent set of rules. As a result, rugby football and 'football' football ('association football') went their separate ways. The rules agreed by the Football Association said, among other things, that you couldn't use your hands unless you were the goalie. Rugby players found this unacceptable.

Fox Talbot, William Henry
pioneer of photography
1800-77

William Fox Talbot didn't invent photography. That honour went to the Frenchman Joseph Niepce back

in 1826. But it was Fox Talbot who invented the process on which all modern photography was based until the start of digital photography. A 'negative' is created and photos are printed from it. The idea came to him while he was sketching, or rather trying to sketch, on Lake Como in Italy. He coated a piece of writing paper in silver chloride and then exposed it to light in a pinhole camera. He developed the image by washing the paper in gallic acid, thus producing a negative from which photos could be printed. He also developed a method of chemically 'fixing' his images so that they would not disappear when exposed to more light.

1835: THE FIRST 'NEGATIVE' WAS OF A WINDOW IN TALBOT'S HOUSE

Fox Talbot worked on his invention for the rest of his life. Among other things, he patented the first photographic enlarger and a method for taking 'instantaneous' photos, and he published the world's first photographically illustrated book, *The Pencil of Nature* (1844-6). He was also a brilliant mathematician, astrologer and chemist and was one of the first people to decipher ancient cuneiform writing from Ninevah in the Middle East.

SOME CUNEIFORM WRITING

franchise, extension of *see* voting

Free Trade
a reasonably realistic recipe for riches

In the eighteenth century, governments didn't want their people to buy and sell the products of other countries. They wanted to protect their own industries. For instance, all the products of the

17 **British Empire** had to be carried on British ships.

Back in 1776, the Scottish thinker Adam Smith had argued that if countries could trade freely with each other, it would be better for everyone. Victorian industrialists liked Smith's idea, especially cotton manufacturers who longed to import cheap American cotton without having to pay import duty*

79 on it. During the 1840s, the government of **Robert Peel** gradually slashed duties on foreign imports into

36 Britain. In 1846 the **Corn Laws** were abolished which had increased the price of foreign grain. As a result of these changes and now that it was easier to import raw materials, British *exports* increased by as much in the next ten years as they had in the previous forty years.

Free Trade worked for Britain, because Britain was

the most industrialised country in the world. By 1850 nearly half of world trade in manufactured goods was British. But British products smashed local craft-based industries, so not everyone welcomed Free Trade. It had to be forced on the Chinese at gunpoint.

Gladstone, William Ewart
seriously a prime minister
1809-98

Two giants towered over Britain in the last half of **Victoria's** reign when the **British Empire** was at the height of its power. One was **Disraeli**, a Tory*, and the other was Gladstone, a Liberal*. Both were Prime Ministers at one time or another, in fact both first became Prime Minister in 1868, and both were brilliant speakers. Victoria preferred Disraeli but Gladstone was in power for longer.

111
17
41

Gladstone started out as a Tory. As a young man he was really quite backward-looking, even by the standards of the day. He even gave a speech at Eton that: education was not 'on the whole' good for the poor!

49

As he grew older his opinions became less right wing. He switched sides and became a Liberal* in the 1850s. As a Liberal, he favoured **free trade** and an increase in the number of working class men who were allowed to vote. Towards the end of his career he backed **Home Rule** for Ireland. Home Rule made him so unpopular with his enemies that he was in danger of assassination.

A seriously religious man, he spent the last few weeks of his life seriously - in prayer.

Gordon, General Charles George
'Chinese Gordon'
he caught it in Khartoum

1833-85

Charles Gordon believed in doing his duty whatever the cost. He first rose to fame in China where he defeated the Taiping rebels in 1863. Gordon's 'Ever Victorious Army' defeated vast numbers of the Taiping, although his force consisted of just 4,000 Chinese soldiers, commanded by a mixed bunch of European officers. The money to pay for their wages and arms came from the Chinese Emperor and various Shanghai merchants.

In 1877 Gordon was made Governor of Sudan, where he fought to suppress the slave trade. (Sudan was then ruled from Egypt which was under British influence.) He retired due to ill health but was asked to return in 1884, when the Sudan was in turmoil due to an uprising led by a fierce leader called 'the Mahdi'. Gordon's job was to arrange for Egyptian civilians and soldiers to leave Sudan and to help set up an independent Sudanese government. In March 1884, Gordon and a small band of defenders were besieged in Khartoum by the Mahdi's army. They held out for ten months. Gordon converted his river steamers into armoured boats and even manufactured land mines. Despite all his efforts, rebel forces entered the city at 3.30 am on Monday 26 January 1885 and he was shot on the steps of the palace. His head was carried to the tent of the Mahdi as a trophy. A rescue expedition from Egypt arrived by river two days later.

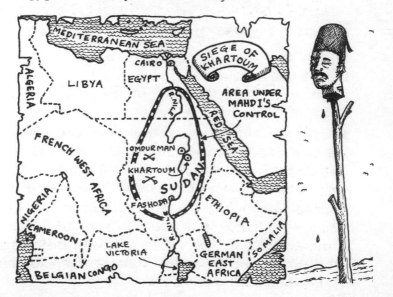

Grace, W.G. (William Gilbert)

cricket legend in his own lifetime

1848-1915

William Grace, 'W.G.' or 'the Champion' as he was known, a Bristol doctor, was the most famous of all Victorian sporting heroes. He was a big, burly man with a big bushy beard. In those days cricket pitches were much rougher than they are today and there were no boundaries. 50 was considered a high score. W.G. usually scored over 100 and often over 200. Huge crowds used to come and watch him play.

Great Exhibition

and greatest greenhouse of all time

1851

In 1851 a huge structure of glass and iron was built in Hyde Park. It was designed by Joseph Paxton, the Duke of Devonshire's estate manager. Paxton's design was chosen by **Prince Albert** himself. It contained 4,572 tons of iron and was clothed in 300,000 panes of glass. This 'Crystal Palace' housed the Great Exhibition, the world's first really major trade exhibition.

The Great Exhibition celebrated the triumph of British power and industry. 13,937 displays from all over the world were seen by more than six million visitors, not just from Britain but from all over Europe as well. From giant steam engines to a garden seat made out of coal, there was something for everyone. The Exhibition was the brainchild of Prince Albert and its success was a triumph for him personally and for the royal family. It was copied by many other countries in the years to come.

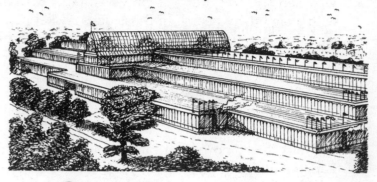

Hardie, James Keir
first labour MP

1856-1915

Keir Hardie was born in a one-room cottage in Lanarkshire, in Scotland. His family were so poor that he had to start work when he was only seven years old. By the age of ten he was working down a mine - he was also studying at night school. In the late 1870s he was able to earn his living as a journalist. Passionately committed to helping the poor, he formed the Scottish Labour Party in 1888.

In 1892 Hardie became the first Independent Labour Member of Parliament, where he scandalised the House of Commons by wearing a working class cloth cap and tweed suit. He became known as 'the member for the unemployed' because he always spoke up for unemployed workers. He went on to help form what became the modern Labour Party. When World War I started he lost heart because he was completely against it. He died a year later.

THE WORKERS SHOULD HAE A SAY IN PARLIAMENT!...

NOO IT'S UP TAE ME!

# Home Rule
campaign for an Irish parliament

In 1801 an 'Act of Union' abolished the Irish Parliament. From then on, Irish MPs sat in the House of Commons and not in Dublin. The Home Rule League was set up by patriotic Irishmen in 1873 to campaign for a parliament based in Dublin to run Irish affairs. In a general election the following year enough Home Rulers were elected to the British Parliament to form an Irish Parliamentary party. From 1875 this party was led by the brilliant, charming and very awkward **Charles Parnell**. 78

49 In 1886 and again in 1893 **William Gladstone** tried to force Home Rule bills through the British Parliament in order to satisfy Parnell's demands. Both times he was defeated by an alliance of Tories* and Irish Protestant MPs who were 'unionists'. That is, they wanted the Act of Union to carry on. Perhaps if Gladstone had had his way, some of the future trouble between Britain and Ireland might have been avoided.

⋋ Indian Mutiny
or national uprising
1857-58

In 1857 a new Enfield rifle was delivered to the British army in India. Before loading, soldiers had to bite off the end of the cartridge. The cartridge was greased with animal fat, probably, but not definitely, a mixture of pork and beef fat - the worst possible mixture. After all, Muslims are forbidden to eat pork and Hindus can't eat beef because to them the cow is a sacred animal. Native Indian soldiers, or 'sepoys' as they were known, objected very strongly, but the army insisted. When sepoys at Meerut were imprisoned for refusing to bite their cartridges, their companions rose up to free them (10 May 1857). Soon the whole of northern India was engulfed in a ferocious rebellion. The doddery, old Mughal emperor was dragged from retirement in Delhi to be their figurehead.

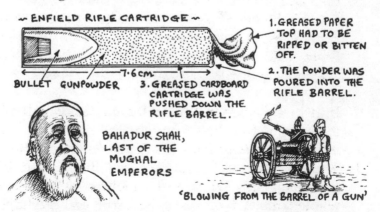

~ ENFIELD RIFLE CARTRIDGE ~

1. GREASED PAPER TOP HAD TO BE RIPPED OR BITTEN OFF.
2. THE POWDER WAS POURED INTO THE RIFLE BARREL.

BULLET   GUNPOWDER   7·6 cm   3. GREASED CARDBOARD CARTRIDGE WAS PUSHED DOWN THE RIFLE BARREL.

BAHADUR SHAH, LAST OF THE MUGHAL EMPERORS

'BLOWING FROM THE BARREL OF A GUN'

The 'Indian Mutiny' was defeated by British soldiers and by Indian troops from other parts of India. There were atrocities by both sides. Especially horrible was the British punishment of 'blowing from the barrel of a gun': captured rebel soldiers were strapped to the barrels of field guns which were then fired.

The 'Mutiny' gave the British a serious shock. When it was over, rule by the East India Company was replaced by direct rule by the British Government.

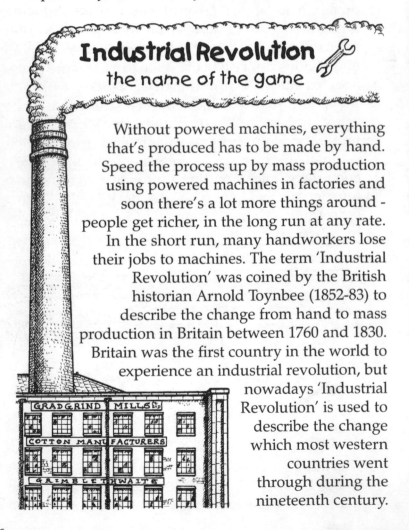

Industrial Revolution
the name of the game

Without powered machines, everything that's produced has to be made by hand. Speed the process up by mass production using powered machines in factories and soon there's a lot more things around - people get richer, in the long run at any rate. In the short run, many handworkers lose their jobs to machines. The term 'Industrial Revolution' was coined by the British historian Arnold Toynbee (1852-83) to describe the change from hand to mass production in Britain between 1760 and 1830. Britain was the first country in the world to experience an industrial revolution, but nowadays 'Industrial Revolution' is used to describe the change which most western countries went through during the nineteenth century.

Inglis, Elsie Maud

woman - and doctor

1864-1917

Elsie Maud Inglis studied medicine in Scotland in the 1890s. Nothing very remarkable about that you might think, but there was - Elsie was a woman, one of the first female medical students in Scotland. Some male doctors objected to the very idea. After she finished her training, she opened a medical school for women in Edinburgh and in 1901 she started a special hospital for women in childbirth which was entirely staffed by women. Later, in 1906, she founded the Scottish Women's Suffragette Federation and during World War I she set up several military hospitals.

Jack the Ripper

nasty man with knife

active 1888

Jack the Ripper prowled the Whitechapel district of London in 1888. At least seven women were his victims. All had their throats cut and their bodies mutilated. No one has ever discovered who Jack was but some people think that he may have been a doctor. He seems to have had some knowledge of human anatomy - a human kidney was mailed to the police during his reign of terror. He's called 'Jack the Ripper' because that's how he signed himself on handwritten notes which he sent to the police. London's chief police commissioner resigned because the police failed to catch him.

Kingsley, Mary Henrietta
female who travelled to foreign places

1862-1900

Mary Kingsley set off on her first voyage in August 1893, to the west coast of Africa. No ordinary tourist, she trudged inland, wading through swamps and marshes and crossing rivers never before seen by European eyes. She came home in January, loaded down with specimens of fish and beetles. By December she was off again, this time to the Congo. During an even more adventurous

journey she climbed the 4,194 metre (13,760 ft) Mungo Mah Lobeh mountain, also called the 'Great Cameroon'. She traded rubber and oil from one place to the next because she didn't have enough money to cover the expenses of her journey.

Mary sailed to South Africa in 1900. The Boer War was still raging and she was set to work nursing sick Boer prisoners. It was probably overwork at this time which killed her.

✎ Kipling, Rudyard
writer who loved an empire
1865-1936

Rudyard Kipling (Rudyard is the name of a Lake in Staffordshire where his parents met) believed in the **British Empire**. He believed that it was the duty of Englishmen to rule less fortunate parts of the world. That's not a fashionable point of view nowadays, but it was then.

17

He was born in British India and returned there in 1882 when he was seventeen to work as a journalist. Within a few years his short stories had made him famous and, although he left India after eight years, he's still remembered as the writer of 'Empire'. Many of his books are still a good read today, including *Kim*, the *Just So Stories*, *Puck of Pook's Hill* and the *Jungle Books*, which the Walt Disney film of the same name is based on.

In later life Kipling became less popular and his later writings are hard to read. He campaigned against votes for women, for conscription* and against democracy in general. One liberal pamphlet called him 'a vindictive maniac'. He lived on through World War I and was saddened to see France, which he loved (and which loved him - his books were almost as popular there as they were in England) so badly damaged by that terrible war.

Kitchener, Horatio Herbert
'Lord Kitchener of Khartoum'
top Victorian soldier

1850-1916

In 1885, Horatio Kitchener was an intelligence officer on the mission to rescue **General Gordon**, then besieged in Khartoum, capital of the Sudan. Back in the Sudan in the 1890s, he led an army against the same Sudanese rebels who had defeated Gordon. The rebels were mown down in their thousands by Kitchener's technically superior force at the Battle of Omdurman (1898), calling to mind the famous rhyme about machine guns:

*Whatever happens, we have got
The Maxim Gun, and they have not.*

RAT TAT TAT
TAT TAT!!
RAT TAT!!

After Omdurman, Kitchener was made 'Baron Kitchener of Khartoum' by **Victoria**. When the **Boer War** broke out in South Africa in 1899, who better than Kitchener to be Chief of Staff to Lord Roberts, the British commander. It was during the Boer War that Kitchener invented concentration camps to hold Boer families captive. They were nothing like as nasty as the German concentration camps of World War I, but 20,000 Boer men, women and children died of disease all the same.

Kitchener was made Secretary of State for War in 1914, when World War I broke out. He died when on a mission to the Czar of Russia, probably when his ship ran into a German mine.

KITCHENER'S FAMOUS
WORLD WAR I POSTER

Lister, Joseph

he started antiseptic surgery

1827-1912

In the early nineteenth century, wounds and cuts often went septic (rotten) overnight. There were no antiseptics to kill germs. Why should there be? germs hadn't been discovered. The only way to treat rot was to chop off the bit which went rotten!

61

Then in 1865, Louis Pasteur discovered that germs, or 'vibrios' as they were first called, cause disease. Joseph Lister was then working as a surgeon at Edinburgh Royal Infirmary where he specialised in treating injuries. Reading about Pasteur's discoveries, Lister saw immediately that it must be germs which caused so many of his patients to die from sepsis. Kill the germs with an *antiseptic* and more of his patients should survive. As his first antiseptic he chose carbolic acid. He treated the skin round wounds, the dressings, his own surgical instruments, everything that might possibly come into contact with a wound. He even sprayed the air with carbolic.

Lister's treatment was brilliantly successful. Death rates fell dramatically. From that time on, it became possible to operate deep within the human body, a type of operation which had previously been thought too dangerous due to the danger of sepsis.

Livingstone, David
explorer of Africa
1813-73

Dr. David Livingstone from Scotland was the greatest of all Victorian explorers and missionaries. He was a good man and he was bitterly opposed to the slave trade. In three great journeys of exploration across the heart of Africa, he 'discovered', among other things, the Victoria Falls, named by him after 111 **Queen Victoria**. Nearly everywhere he went he won the affection of the local people.

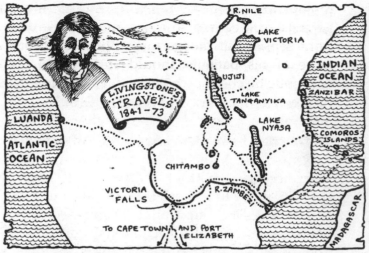

In 1866, he set out to discover the source of the River Nile. He'd always been very tough (he was once attacked by a lion and survived), but this journey was the toughest of the lot. Years went by and nothing was heard of him. Eventually the journalist 100 **Henry Morton Stanley** was sent out to find him and they met at Ujiji on the banks of Lake Tanganyika, where Stanley is said to have greeted him with the famous words: 'Doctor Livingstone, I presume.' The two men became friends. But although he was so sick that he had to be carried on a litter, Livingstone refused to return home with Stanley. He pressed on into the unknown and finally died at Chitambo (in modern Zambia). His African followers wrapped his body in bark and sent it back to Britain. His heart they buried in Africa.

Manchester Ship Canal

short cut for cotton

Nineteenth-century Manchester was the cotton capital of the world. But Manchester is inland and most of the world is overseas. Finished Manchester textiles had to be transported overland to the port of Liverpool where they could be loaded onto ships to be taken to the four corners of the world.

The overland transport was costly and slowed things down, so the Manchester merchants decided that they needed a port of their own. If Manchester couldn't move to the sea, then the sea must come to Manchester. The Ship Canal was opened 1894. It's a deep-water channel, deep enough to take ocean-going vessels, which runs for thirty-six miles from the Mersey Estuary into the heart of Manchester.

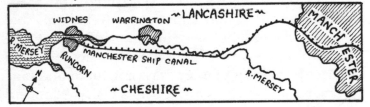

Married Women's Property Act

when married women got their money back

1870s

In the old days, when a woman married a man, he was the boss and he took control of all her property and wealth, even if she was far richer than he was.

For a man, marrying a rich heiress was a bit like winning the lottery.

The system worked reasonably well if the husband was a decent chap who cared for and respected his wife. Unfortunately, not all men are **HAH!** decent chaps. A married woman whose husband was a rotter was in a terribly weak position. He could spend all her money and there was nothing she could do about it. **BAH!**

The 1857 Divorce Act gave divorced and separated women control of their property. It was a start, but not enough. A 'Married Women's Property Committee' was formed (1868) to campaign for more. As a result of their efforts, laws passed in 1870, 1878 and 1882 gave all married women full control over their own wages and property.

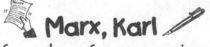

Marx, Karl
founder of communism

1818-83

Karl Marx, a German Jew, was horrified by the
conditions of workers in the new factories and mines of the **Industrial Revolution**. In 1849 he moved to London to escape arrest for his revolutionary activities in Europe. He wrote the *Communist Manifesto** (1848) for a group of exiled German craftsmen, who like him were fighting for political

change. In the *Communist Manifesto*, Marx explained why the world was divided into rich and poor and what the working class could do to change things. His theory became known as 'Marxism' and was one of the most important political theories the world has ever known. Some countries such as China still call themselves Marxist.

Marx said that all history is based on struggles between different classes. New technologies bring new classes to power. Once, tribal chiefs ruled, then came medieval kings, and so on. In his time, capitalists, the owners of factories and other sources of wealth, had the power. The latest struggle was between capitalists and their workers - and the workers would win in the long run. As far as workers were concerned it was a gospel of hope.

Marx eked out a living by writing articles for newspapers. He spent long hours in the reading room of the British Museum where he wrote his great book, *Das Kapital*, and other works. He's buried in Highgate Cemetery in London.

Maxwell, James Clerk
Scotsman who fielded a force
1831-79

James Clerk Maxwell was a brilliant Scottish mathematician and scientist. His 'field equations' described a universe which seemed very strange and abstract to people used to the solid certainties of Victorian Britain. Maxwell's universe was a weird place, criss-crossed by an invisible web of electromagnetic fields and forces.

What Maxwell had done was to describe Faraday's laws of electromagnetism in mathematical terms (Faraday was a hopeless mathematician). Working at Cambridge in the years 1864-73, he proved beyond doubt what Faraday had suggested - that electricity and magnetism must always exist together, that they're two sides of the same coin. He showed that light itself is a form of electromagnetic radiation.

Mill, John Stuart

he had reasons for being unreasonable

1806-73

John Stuart Mill was perhaps the greatest Victorian philosopher. According to Mill, we're not born with any particular powers of reason except for basic 'enumerative induction'. Enumerative induction allows us to work out basic rules from repeated experiences. For instance, if we see lots of cats catching and eating their prey, we are able to assume that cats eat meat. (A useful thing to be able to do when it comes to tigers.)

Mill was a 'utilitarian': he believed that the aim of society should be 'the greatest possible good for the greatest possible number', an idea first spelled out by the English philosopher Jeremy Bentham in the eighteenth century. Mill believed that the 'greatest possible good' must include equality between men and women, and also the greatest possible freedom for individuals, that, in his words:

The only purpose for which power can be rightfully exercised over any member of a civilised community, against his will, is to prevent harm to others.

...LIBERTY CONSISTS IN DOING WHAT ONE DESIRES...

PROBABLY!

It's a difficult philosophy to swallow if you're a modern supporter of safety laws, such as the compulsory wearing of seat belts in cars and of helmets on motorbikes, to name but two. But Mill wasn't modern and there weren't many Victorian safety laws.

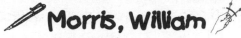 Morris, William

craftsman and socialist

1834-96

William Morris believed that the factories of the 56 **Industrial Revolution** had robbed workers of their dignity and he tried to show how things could be different. He and a few friends started the 'Arts and Crafts' movement. They made beautiful things by 84 hand. They and their artistic friends in the **Pre-Raphaelite Movement** looked back to a time before the Industrial Revolution for their inspiration. Much of their work has a medieval feel, but with a modern, or rather, a Victorian, edge to it. In his most famous books *A Dream of John Ball*, *The Earthly Paradise* and *News from Nowhere*, Morris wrote of an England which was both socialist and sort of medieval at the same time.

Morris's designs influenced the modern world in more ways than he intended. These days, William

Morris wallpaper is mass-produced in factories. And the mass-built houses on most modern British estates owe the modern origin of their 'traditional' look to the 'Red House', a beautiful house designed for Morris in 1859.

~ THE RED HOUSE, BEXLEY, KENT (DESIGNED 1859) ~

music hall and theatre
things to do in the evening

Imagine a life without television or cinema - if you can. In Victorian times, people had to go out to the theatre or music hall to get their entertainment. Theatre was amazingly popular, especially on a Saturday night. There were posh theatres for listening to Shakespeare or opera, and cheap theatres for listening to 'melodramas'. Melodramas had over-dramatic plots with lots of violence, crime and strong emotion. It was sensible to queue early if you wanted to get a decent seat.

Even cheaper than cheap theatres were the 'penny gaffs'. The entertainers usually performed on makeshift stages in empty rooms above shops, and the audiences were often children. The first music hall, 'The Canterbury', opened in London in 1851. Music halls put on mixed performances where popular songs, comic acts, patriotic songs and other acts such as juggling took turns on the stage. The audience sang along in the choruses and shouted coarse jokes at the performers. Music halls were very lively places and the bar was almost as important as the stage. Soon they were as popular as the theatre.

Nasmyth, James
he forged a steam hammer
1808-90

James Nasmyth, a Scottish engineer, invented the steam hammer. Before the steam hammer, iron foundries had to hammer hot metal into shape by hand, so the craftsman's strength set a limit to the size of objects which could be forged and to how quickly they could be made. Massive steam-powered hammers made iron works far more productive.

Nasmyth dreamt up the idea in 1839, when he was asked to forge a massive shaft for the paddles of the steamship, *Great Britain*, designed by **Isambard Brunel**.

21

The idea came to him in a flash of inspiration. It took just half an hour to jot it down in his 'scheme book'. As things turned out, Brunel decided to use newly-invented propellers on his ship so the shaft was never made.

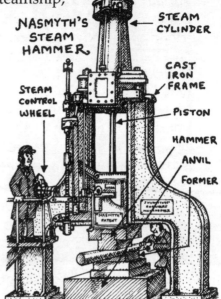

NASMYTH'S STEAM HAMMER

STEAM CYLINDER

CAST IRON FRAME

STEAM CONTROL WHEEL

PISTON

HAMMER

ANVIL

FORMER

Newman, Cardinal *see* Oxford Movement

Nightingale, Florence
the 'Lady of the Lamp'
mother of modern nursing
1820-1910

Florence Nightingale (named after Florence in Italy where she was born) had wealthy parents. As a small girl she dreaded the restricted lifestyle which would be her destiny as an upper-class Victorian woman. She was determined to do something useful. The useful thing that Florence decided to do was to make British nursing a 'calling' to be proud of.

Her big chance came in 1854 when the **Crimean War** broke out. Wounded British soldiers were appallingly treated, causing a scandal back in London. The Secretary of State for War, who was a friend of the Nightingales, asked Florence to go out and help. She arrived at the British military hospital in Scutari (now a suburb of Istanbul) a month later with a party of forty-six nuns and nurses plus all their equipment.

The army hospital at Scutari was a hell hole. Men lay on their bunks and on the floor caked in grime and gore. The food was almost inedible. They were dying like flies. Florence organised decent nursing, a huge kitchen and a laundry. She worked twenty hours a day to get things started. She allowed no other woman to visit the wards after eight at night, patrolling the darkened rooms alone. In gratitude for her care the soldiers called her the 'Lady of the Lamp'.

The death rate reached 45% in 1855, but after that, mainly due to Florence's efforts, it fell to 2%. The worst was over. When she returned to England in August 1856 she was a popular hero. **Victoria** gave her a brooch designed by **Albert**. By the time she died, nursing was indeed a calling to be proud of - as it still is today.

⚔ Opium Wars
how the Chinese were paid for tea
1839-41 & 1857-58

The British like tea, huge quantities of it. In the late eighteenth century China tea was what they drank. Unfortunately, the Chinese didn't seem to want or need anything British in return. The tea trade was a drain on British resources. To counter this, the British began to grow tea in India, and they also discovered opium. Opium grown in British India was shipped illegally to China and sold for Chinese silver. The silver was then used (indirectly) to buy tea. By the 1830s, thousands of Chinese had become addicted to opium. Now the British had something the Chinese wanted even more than the British wanted tea - a neat solution to their problem.

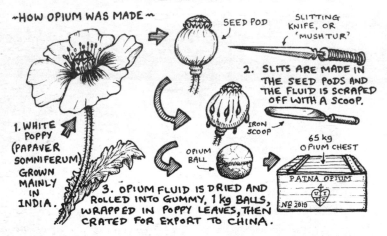

~HOW OPIUM WAS MADE~

SEED POD

SLITTING KNIFE, OR 'MUSHTUR'

2. SLITS ARE MADE IN THE SEED PODS AND THE FLUID IS SCRAPED OFF WITH A SCOOP.

IRON SCOOP

1. WHITE POPPY (PAPAVER SOMNIFERUM) GROWN MAINLY IN INDIA.

OPIUM BALL

65 kg OPIUM CHEST

PATNA OPIUM

Nº 2819

3. OPIUM FLUID IS DRIED AND ROLLED INTO GUMMY, 1 kg BALLS, WRAPPED IN POPPY LEAVES, THEN CRATED FOR EXPORT TO CHINA.

The Chinese government didn't agree. In 1839, the top Chinese offical in Canton, Lin Tse-hsü, ordered that 20,000 chests of best British opium be burned, the remains to be thrown in the Pearl River. Meanwhile British merchants were besieged in their warehouse complex at Canton for several weeks, before retreating to Hong Kong. The British government sent out a force of soldiers. After two years of war, China agreed to pay compensation for the lost opium and, as an extra, ceded Hong Kong to Britain (Treaty of Nanking, 1842).

The trade in opium didn't grow as expected. The British were disappointed. Meanwhile the Chinese, far from acting beaten, became very hostile to foreigners. In the second Opium War (1857-58) the British joined forces with the French and beat the Chinese yet again. At the Treaty of Tientsin (1859), the Chinese agreed to three key demands: Christian missionaries were free to preach their faith, British and other representatives could live all year round in Peking - and opium was legalised.

Oxford Movement

it changed the Church of England

Roman Catholics burn incense and hang paintings in their churches. Roman Catholic priests perform elaborate rituals dressed in priestly garments. Protestants on the other hand have no incense, few paintings, simple rituals and the ministers dress simply.

So why can you smell incense during so many Church of England services nowadays, and why do so many Church of England vicars wear Catholic-style priestly garments? The Church of England is a Protestant church - isn't it?

The answer lies in the Oxford Movement, begun at Oxford University in 1833 by John Henry Newman and a group of like-minded friends. Also known as 'Tractarians' because they published their opinions in a series of ninety 'Tracts for Our Times', they set out to turn the Church of England into a more Catholic sort of church. In fact Newman went the whole hog. In 1845, he joined the Roman Catholics. He was made 'Cardinal Newman' by a grateful pope in 1879.

Palmerston, Lord Henry John Temple

he gave us gunboat diplomacy

1784-1865

Lord Palmerston, Third Viscount Temple, was a toff. He was handsome and rich and he liked smart clothes. Like many men of his class he believed that it was his duty to help govern the country. He was Foreign Secretary (1830-41 and 1846-51) then Home Secretary, and finally Prime Minister (1855-8 and 1859-65). During his long career he was nearly always popular because, as well as being clever and rich, he was generous, never bore grudges and had a good sense of humour.

Palmerston was never Tory* enough for the Tories nor Liberal* enough for the Liberals. He had his own opinions. As Foreign Secretary, for which he's most famous, he used 'gunboat diplomacy' (i.e. the power of the Royal Navy) when it was useful, 17 loathed the slave trade, believed in the **British Empire** and distrusted Russia. He was at the heart of 74 55 power during the **Opium Wars**, the **Indian Mutiny**, 37 the **Crimean War** and the American Civil War.

Parnell, Charles Stewart

Irishman who pestered Parliament

1846-91

In Victorian times there was no Irish parliament. Since 1801 Irish MPs had sat in the House of  Commons in England. Parnell led the fight for '**Home Rule**'. He wanted an Irish Parliament in Dublin to rule Ireland. Ireland would be part of the **British Empire** but separate, like Canada.

Starting in 1875, he forged the Irish MPs in the House of Commons into a strong, organised group. They set out to force the government to grant Home Rule - by clogging up the government, a technique called 'filibustering'. They dragged out every debate and argued every point of every bill, however absurd. On and on they droned. Some debates lasted for more than forty-eight hours non-stop. It was dreadful.

Parnell also campaigned for land reform. Irish farmers were desperately poor and they were often evicted from their farms when they couldn't pay their rent. Parnell advised 'Boycotting', named after its first victim, Captain Charles Boycott. Any Irishman who took over a farm from which the previous tenant had been evicted was to be shunned by his community.

49 Finally Prime Minister **Gladstone** agreed to Home Rule. Unfortunately, Protestant Liberals* from Ireland changed sides and backed the Tories* to defeat Gladstone. There was no Home Rule. Parnell meanwhile had been having an affair with Mrs Kitty O'Shea, the wife on one of his Irish MPs. In 1889, Captain O'Shea asked for a divorce and stated Parnell as the reason. Parnell later married Kitty, but the scandal ruined his career.

 # Peel, Robert
he planned a police force
1788-1850

Robert Peel could work for up to sixteen hours a day, day after day without tiring and was also a brilliant speaker. He dominated the Tory* Party at the start of **Victoria's** reign and was Prime Minister twice, 1834-5 and 1841-6. Peel had realised that if Britain was to avoid the revolutions which swept Europe in the mid-nineteenth century, there would have to be reform at home. And reform would have to start with his own party. It was Peel who changed the old Tory Party into the modern mass membership Conservative Party.

Due to Protestant fears, British Catholics had been

forbidden to sit in Parliament or hold any other public office since the seventeenth century. Peel emancipated* the Roman Catholics. Nowadays, about the only thing a British Catholic can't do is to become king or queen.

> HOW DOES IT GO?.. AH! I REMEMBER..

> WHAT'S ALL THIS 'ERE, THEN?..

> LET'S BE HAVING YOU!..

> HAVE YOU EVER BEEN IN TROUBLE BEFORE?..

> NOW THEN, NOW THEN!..

> ER...

48 Peel also believed in **Free Trade**. It was because of this that he repealed the

36 **Corn Laws** in 1846, allowing foreign imports into the country. Back in 1829, as Home Secretary, he set up the Metropolitan Police Force, the first proper police force in Britain - thus 'bobby', a slang name for a policeman, from his forename 'Robert'.

EARLY UNIFORM OF ONE OF ROBERT PEEL'S 'BOBBIES'

Peel was a proud man. He once challenged the Irish leader Daniel O'Connell to a duel. He died after a fall from his horse while riding on Constitution Hill in London.

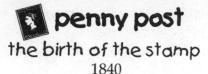

penny post
the birth of the stamp
1840

Before the penny post was introduced, posting letters could be a nightmare. The further your letter had to travel, the more you paid. An Irish labourer working in England had to pay a fifth of a week's wages to send a letter home - if he paid at all, that is. Most letters were paid for on delivery. Poor families lived in dread of having to find money for letters sent to them unexpectedly.

Rowland Hill worked out that the transport of letters made up only a small fraction of the total cost of delivering them. The system of charges was so complicated that most of the cost came from paying the wages of the people who worked out how much to charge! Hill suggested a single rate of one penny per half ounce (14 grams) no matter where in the country a letter was delivered, all postage to be prepaid with sticky stamps bought from the Post Office. Hill's Penny Post was introduced in 1840. By

1868 when he retired from the Post Office (he was given a job there in 1847), the number of letters posted per year had risen from 76 million to 642 million. All this and the cost of sending letters had fallen to a fraction of what it had been before.

political parties
not a balloon in sight

The Victorian period gave birth to two large political babies: the Conservative Party baby and the Liberal* Party baby (from which in turn the modern Labour Party was born).

The Conservatives were formed from the old Tory* 79 party around 1834, mainly by **Robert Peel** (the word 'conservative' to describe them was first used in 54 1830). After the **Home Rule** crisis of 1886 and 1893 a group of Irish MPs split with the Liberals and joined the Conservatives to form the 'Conservative and Unionist Party'. Victorian Conservatives believed in respect for authority and the crown, strengthening 17 the **British Empire** and keeping things roughly as they were.

The other baby, the Liberals, grew after the reform Bill of 1832, when rich middle class gentlemen began to join Parliament in increasing numbers. The newcomers teamed up with the old Whig aristocrats 77 such as **Lord Palmerston**, since both groups were interested in reforming the country. By 1839 the old Whigs and the new intake were all being referred to 48 as 'Liberals'. Liberals believed in **Free Trade** and reform of the voting system among other things. The first proper Liberal government is said to have been formed by Lord Russell in 1840. From 1865 the party 49 was dominated by **William Gladstone**.

population

In the nineteenth century the population of Britain increased from 16 million to over 40 million, despite massive emigration to America, Canada, Australia and South Africa.

Potato Famine (Irish)
starvation in Ireland
1845-49

Traditionally an Irish farmer's land was divided up between all his sons when he died, instead of all of it going to the eldest son as in England. This meant that farms became smaller and smaller with each generation. The potato is ideal for a very small farm with many mouths to feed, because potatoes are very nourishing and lots of potatoes can be grown on a small patch of land. By the 1840s nearly half of the Irish population ate almost nothing else.

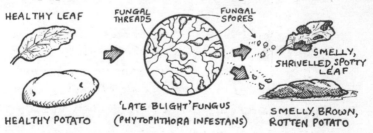

HEALTHY LEAF

FUNGAL THREADS

FUNGAL SPORES

SMELLY, SHRIVELLED SPOTTY LEAF

HEALTHY POTATO

'LATE BLIGHT' FUNGUS (PHYTOPHTHORA INFESTANS)

SMELLY, BROWN, ROTTEN POTATO

All well and good - if the crop doesn't fail. Starting in 1845 the Irish potato crop was repeatedly destroyed by 'late blight' caused by a fungus from America. The result was mass starvation which reached its peak in the winter of 1846-7. To start with the British government under **Robert Peel** tried hard to help, but then the government changed. In 1846, the new

79

Liberal* government under Lord John Russell said that there had to be a purely Irish solution to the problem and refused (for a while) to stop the export of food from Ireland as being against **Free Trade**. Good food was shipped out of the country because the starving Irish were too poor to pay for it. Government soup kitchens were set up but they were never enough to stop the deaths.

48

Up to 1,100,000 people died during the Potato Famine and as many as 1.5 million may have emigrated in 'coffin ships', mainly to the USA. The population of Ireland fell from 8,400,000 in the 1840s to 6,600,000 in 1851. Irish bitterness resulting from the Potato Famine helped to fuel Irish demands for independence.

Pre-Raphaelite Brotherhood ✎
painters who delighted in detail

'High art' in the early nineteenth century was 'classical' - it was based on ideas of beauty developed by the ancient Greeks. Worship of all things classical had first taken root in Renaissance Italy in the late Middle Ages. Raphael (1483-1520) was one of the greatest Italian renaissance painters.

In 1848, three young art students at the Royal Academy - Holman Hunt, John Everett Millais and Dante Gabriel Rossetti - joined together to form the Pre-Raphaelite Brotherhood. They were against the fashionable, classical style of painting and they didn't like the paintings of Raphael. Their paintings were going to look to the real Middle Ages, to the period of Italian art before Raphael. Others joined them, including later the gifted artists **William Morris**, Ford Madox Brown and Edward Burne-Jones. To begin with the Pre-Raphaelite Brotherhood exhibited their paintings under the initials PRB only.

Pre-Raphaelite paintings are very detailed with bright, almost picture-postcard colours, on subjects which are usually medieval or religious or both. You can see Pre-Raphaelite works in the municipal galleries of major industrial cities such as Birmingham, Liverpool and Manchester.

prison
a solitary experience

The last convict ship to sail to Australia left port in 1867. From then on British criminals had to be kept in prison in Britain. The Victorians had a very harsh attitude towards prison. Prisoners were kept isolated from each other in small cells. When led from their cells they often had to wear a brown cotton mask with eyeholes so that their fellow prisoners wouldn't recognise them. Contact between prisoners, even a glance, was often forbidden.

The men had to spend their days on pointless or monotonous tasks, such as pacing the tread mill, a large heavy wheel which went nowhere, or unpicking ropes to make oakum - which nobody wanted. Savage punishments such as whippings or the strait-jacket were dealt out if anyone broke the rules. By the end of the century, small improvements had been made to the standard prison regime, but men still left prison more bitter and twisted than when they went in.

public schools *see* schools

Pugin, Augustus Welby Northmore

he helped design Parliament

1812-52

There's nothing worth living for but Christian architecture and a boat.

Gothic architecture is the style of architecture of most churches and cathedrals. It became very popular in the Victorian period. Pugin designed a large number of Gothic churches and other buildings. He also designed a house for himself with a built-in church at Ramsgate, near the sea because sailing was his other passion. He became a Roman Catholic and spent a lot of time in religious ritual in his private church. Overwork unhinged his mind and he ended up in Bedlam, the London mad house, dying shortly after.

Pugin is most famous for his designs for the Houses of Parliament, drawings which he started in 1836 and took seven years to complete. The architect Charles Barry was responsible for the overall concept but it was Pugin who designed the details and the interiors.

railways *see* **transport**

Reform Acts *see* **voting**

Rhodes, Cecil
Empire builder in Africa

1853-1902

Cecil Rhodes, the son of a vicar from Hertfordshire, made a huge fortune from diamond mining in South Africa, in the 1870s. His company, later called 'De Beers' after the Boer farmer who once owned the land above the mine, now controls much of the world's diamond industry.

Rhodes was more than a miner. He believed that it was Britain's duty to rule the world. After his first heart attack in 1877, he wrote a will donating all his wealth to a 'Secret Society founded to extend British rule throughout the world'. Once Britain ruled the world, there would be no further wars and all countries could prosper in peace.

Rhodes became immensely powerful in southern Africa and was Prime Minister of what was then called the Cape Colony in 1891-5. Nothing came of his secret society, but through his British South African Company founded in 1889, he acquired vast territories from African rulers in what are now Zambia and Zimbabwe. This huge area was called Rhodesia in his honour and was a British colony for many years.

Roman Catholic emancipation
Catholics come in from the cold

In the fifteenth and sixteenth centuries, British Roman Catholics* had been stamped on as enemies of the state. Among other things, they couldn't buy land, vote, sit in Parliament, go to university, join the army or hold government jobs. These restrictions were gradually lifted, but it wasn't until 1829 that the Emancipation Act gave them political equality with Protestants*. The act allowed them to sit in Parliament and hold government jobs. Finally in 1871, Catholics were allowed to go to university.

Nowadays only one law discriminates against Catholics in Britain - they're not allowed to be king or queen.

✏ Ruskin, John
Victorian art guru
1819-1900

Britain in the nineteenth century went through huge
56 changes due to the **Industrial Revolution**. New railway lines cut through the landscape, ugly modern cities sprang up, factory chimneys smeared the sky with smoke. Many people looked back longingly to a time before all the ugliness started. That was why Victorian architects built so many buildings in the Gothic style of medieval churches,
84 why the **Pre-Raphaelites** painted medieval scenes and why romantic artists such as William Turner often chose dramatic natural scenes for

their paintings. John Ruskin was a writer and thinker who defended Turner, the Pre-Raphaelites and Gothic architecture against their critics. His books, especially *Modern Painters* and *The Stones of Venice*, dictated fashions in art for more than a generation.

Salisbury, Robert Arthur, Lord

old-fashioned Prime Minister

1830-1903

Lord Salisbury was a conservative. He believed that: 'It is better to endure almost any political evil than to risk a breach of the historical continuity of government.'

In other words, keep things as they are at all costs - a very sensible belief for a rich English nobleman at the height of the Victorian age. In 1881 after **Disraeli** died, he became leader of the conservatives and was Prime Minster twice. He retired in 1902, having led Britain through the **Boer War**.

Salisbury opposed nearly all the great reforms of the nineteenth century. He opposed **Home Rule**, the repeal of the **Corn Laws** and the extension of the right to vote to more people. He was particularly opposed to democracy. Back in 1867 he very nearly retired from public life because he came to understand that his opinions were 'of the past'.

Salvation Army

they battled against despair

William Booth was a fiery preacher from a poor Nottingham family. In 1865 he opened a 'Christian Mission' in the poorest part of the East End of

London. With his wife Catherine, a clever invalid who spent most of her time on the sofa, and his son Bramwell, he forged his mission into a worldwide organisation.

Booth's mission took the name 'Salvation Army' in 1878, although Booth himself was rather against it, even though he was given the title 'General for Life'. Nowadays the Salvation Army is organised into corps under officers rising from lieutenant to brigadier (the officers are really ministers). New recruits sign 'Articles of War', they wear a uniform and sell their newspaper *War Cry* on the streets. But their war is on poverty and to save souls for Christ - guns have nothing to do with it.

 schools

something for almost everyone

In 1851, less than half of Britain's children went to school. A lot more of them could have gone to school but didn't. Either they were out working to help support their families or they were, well - out. Large gangs of children running wild in the streets were a common sight. This went on until 1880, when school was made compulsory. There was a surprisingly wide range of schools on offer for those who did get an education: 'ragged' schools for very poor children, dame schools usually run by a local woman, part-time factory schools, Sunday schools, and private day schools which cost more.

For the middle and upper classes there were public schools - large boarding schools where bullying and beating were common. A public school education was vital for young men who wanted to climb the social ladder, so public schools sprang up like mushrooms to meet the demand. Public schoolboys played a lot of sport and were taught mainly Latin and Greek.

The first Victorian private school for girls, Queen's College London, was opened in 1847. Demand for girls' education grew quickly. By 1871 the first women's university college, Newnham College Cambridge, had been founded.

⚒ servants
summoned by bells

There were more servants in Victorian Britain than any other type of worker. Wages were so low that even quite humble middle class families could afford at least one maid to help with the housework. In fact, it was considered rather shameful not to be able to afford any servants at all. The very wealthy had armies of them to tend to their houses and estates. Senior servants such as the butler and the housekeeper had a lot of responsibility and numbers of other servants working for them. But most servants were at the mercy of their employers and, while some employers were kind and thoughtful, many more forced their servants to work very long hours and to be at their beck and call from morning to night.

In large houses, the servants' living and working quarters were usually in the basements 'below stairs', separated from the family by a door covered in green baize cloth. The family would call for them by means of elaborate systems of bells which were sounded by bell ropes which hung in most rooms. The maids often slept in small rooms under the roof.

Sevastopol, fall of *see* **Crimean War**

Shaftesbury, Lord
(Cooper, Anthony Ashley)
kind-hearted reformer
1801-85

Lord Shaftesbury had it all: he was good looking, noble and clever. If he'd wanted to he might well have become Prime Minister at some stage in his career. But, although he was a Member of Parliament, he was more interested in doing good than in gaining power. He worked to improve the treatment of the mentally ill, at a time when they were treated

little better than circus freaks. He was also a leading figure behind the **Factories Acts** which improved working conditions in factories and textile mills - it was Shaftesbury who introduced the Ten Hours Bill limiting the working hours of women and children to ten hours maximum per day. He was also behind an act forbidding the employment of women and young children underground in the mines, where they were often very badly treated. Another of his acts was one to improve conditions for 'climbing boys', young chimney sweeps employed to climb up the chimneys in great Victorian houses.

Simpson, Sir James Young

doctor who first used chloroform

1801-70

In the 1840s, there was no way of dulling the pain of operations. About the only thing a patient could do was to get blind drunk beforehand. In 1846 Doctor Simpson heard about the use of ether by American doctors and dentists as an anaesthetic - to make their patients unconscious. At that time it was fashionable to remove all of a patient's teeth at one sitting so as to provide them with a complete set of false teeth, so ether was very welcome.

Simpson thought that there might be a better anaesthetic than ether. He and two assistants experimented on themselves by sniffing various substances until one day all three woke up under the table. They had sniffed chloroform, the first really useful anaesthetic. To start with, many people thought that all anaesthetics, chloroform in particular, were a danger to health and against the will of God who must have

given us pain for a reason. But the advantages were overwhelming. Soon chloroform was being used in hospitals all over the world. Chloroform can be quite dangerous and nowadays new and far better anaesthetics are available. But we have Simpson to thank for this vital step forward in medicine.

slavery, abolition of 👉
the end of a curse

For much of the eighteenth century British merchants worked the 'triangular trade' - goods were sold to African rulers in exchange for African slaves, the slaves were shipped across the Atlantic, and sold for sugar, cotton and other American goods, which were then shipped back to Britain. Liverpool, Bristol and other British ports grew fat on the profits.

But there was a problem. Britain itself had no slavery. As far back as 1569, Queen Elizabeth I had stated: 'England is too pure an air for slaves to breathe in'. So there was always a current of British opinion which disliked the trade. From 1772, and often before that, escaped slaves were free if they could reach British soil.

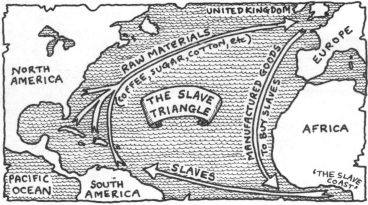

In Britain the anti-slavery movement was led at first by William Wilberforce, a wealthy philanthropist and by the Quakers* but it soon gained widespread support. In 1807 Britain abolished the slave trade with her colonies and then set out to stop other people from slaving. Royal navy ships prowled the Atlantic on the lookout for slavers. The last bastion of slavery in the British Empire fell in 1834 when slavery was finally abolished in the British West Indies.

Somerville, Mary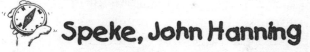
famous woman scientist

1780-1872

Mary Somerville was a writer about science and also a scientist, although it is as a writer that she's best known. During her lifetime she was one of the most respected women of her generation. Somerville College in Oxford, the first Oxford college for women, is named after her.

Speke, John Hanning
'discoverer' of the source of the Nile

1827-64

In 1856, John Speke joined an expedition led by 22 **Richard Burton** to explore a lake in East Africa said to lie to the east of what is now Kenya. They reached what is now called Lake Tanganyika early in 1858 after many adventures. Burton was so ill that Speke explored the lake on his own in a canoe. That June, because Burton was still ill, Speke set off in search of another larger lake to the north. Thus it was that Speke became the first European to set eyes on Lake

Victoria, named after the Queen. He immediately decided that this lake was the source of the River Nile.

When the expedition returned to the African coast, Burton was too ill to travel back to England straight away. Speke returned alone. By the time Burton got back, Speke had claimed most of the credit for the expedition and had arranged for another expedition to Lake Victoria to be commanded by himself.

On 25 September 1860, Speke left Zanzibar at the head of a large expedition of 217 men including porters. He explored Lake Victoria thoroughly and saw where the Nile flowed out of it. He then followed the Nile all the way north to Egypt. Burton could never bring himself to accept that Speke was right about the Nile flowing out of Lake Victoria. A special debate between the two men was arranged for 15 September 1864 at a conference of the British Association for the Advancement of Science in Bath. Unfortunately Speke accidentally shot himself while shooting partridge on the morning of the debate, so the two explorers never got to discuss their disagreement in public.

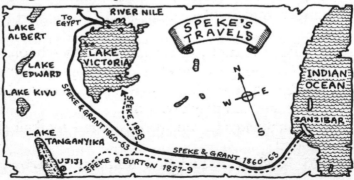

sport
recreation as a rule

Victorian schoolboys were sport mad. It was said that a keen cricketer at Eton in the early part of the century could play cricket for up to twenty-one hours per week. When the schoolboys left school, they carried their sports mania into the big wide world where others soon copied them. Especially the industrial working class, who took up football and turned it into the massive game it is today.

The difference between earlier sports and modern sport as invented by the Victorians lies in the rules, rules which allowed sportsmen and women to compete fairly with each other:

1846 Rules of rugby published at Rugby school.
1848 Cambridge football rules attempt to combine rules by which football is played at different schools so that they can play each other.
1855 Sheffield FC, the world's oldest football club, founded.
46 1863 **Football Association** founded - rugby and

football finally part company.

1866 London Athletic Club founded - the first athletics club.

1866 8th Marquis of Queensberry helps to produce the 'Queensberry Rules' for boxing.

1870s Rules of snooker devised by British Army officers based in India.

1875 Marylebone Cricket Club publishes revised, standardised rules for tennis.

1880 Amateur Athletic Association founded.

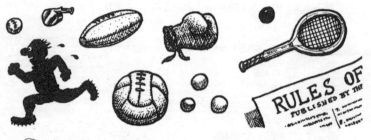

Stanley, Sir Henry Morton
Welsh explorer in Africa

1841-1904

John Rowlands's father died when he was only two. His mother went to be a servant in London, one lot of grandparents refused to have anything to do with him and the other lot paid a measly pittance for him to be looked after by an old couple in Denbigh.

Four years later young John was sent to the workhouse. Eventually he ran away and sailed to America as a cabin boy. There he was befriended by a kindly, New Orleans cotton merchant called Henry Stanley, who later adopted him.

AMERICA HERE I COME!

John Rowlands changed his name to Henry Morton Stanley in honour of his adoptive father who later died. After countless adventures, including fighting in the American Civil War, being taken prisoner, shipwreck and campaigns among native Americans, Stanley ended up as a reporter for the *New York Herald*. He was a brilliant reporter. In 1871 he was told by Gordon Bennett (the owner of the newspaper) to go and find the famous explorer 62 **David Livingstone** who was lost somewhere in Africa and to bring him back.

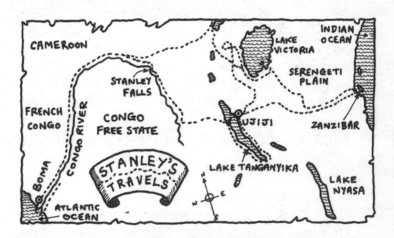

Stanley found Livingstone at Ujiji on the shore of Lake Tanganyika and the two men became friends. They explored the lake together. But Livingstone refused to return with Stanley and stayed on in Africa to die. Stanley returned with the story of a lifetime but no Livingstone. From 1874-7 he traced the mighty River Congo from its source in East Africa to the Atlantic Ocean, and in 1879 he founded the Congo Free State for the King of Belgium (a disaster for the native Africans).

Stephenson, George

inventor of the first useful steam train

1781-1848

Before the coming of the railways, the fastest anyone could travel was the speed of a galloping horse. By the time George Stephenson retired you could travel from London to Newcastle by train in just nine hours, at an average speed of approximately 28 mph. It was Stephenson, the son of a fireman in the Northumberland mines, more than anyone else, who created the British railway system.

Stephenson invented the flanged wheel which is common to all modern railway systems, as well as many improvements to steam engine design. His greatest project, the design of the Manchester to Liverpool railway and of the 'Rocket', the steam train which ran on it, was finished in 1829, before **Victoria** came to the throne. Before he retired in 1845 he had designed most of the railways which connect the major cities of the north of England.

111

Stevenson, Robert Louis Balfour

children's adventure writer

1850-94

One of the most successful shilling thrillers of all time was *The Strange Case of Dr Jekyll and Mr Hyde* by

Robert Louis Stevenson, published in 1886, an extraordinary tale of murder and split personalities.

Stevenson was one of the most popular writers of his generation. His first bestseller, *Treasure Island*, a story of pirates and buried treasure, was published in 1883. It was followed by a string of other bestsellers, including *A Child's Garden of Verses* (1885) and *Kidnapped* (1886) which is also about pirates.

Stevenson was Scottish and loved Scotland. Unfortunately he suffered from bad lung disease and the damp Scottish climate was the worst possible thing for it. In 1887 he set sail for the South Pacific, together with most of his family. They set up home on the beautiful island of Samoa and for the remaining years of his life Stevenson's health stayed moderately good. But eventually even the sunny climate of Samoa couldn't save him. He's buried on the summit of Mount Vaea in the centre of the island.

Swan, Joseph Wilson
he invented a light bulb

1828-1914

Joseph Swan was a chemist from Newcastle who designed an early electric light bulb back in 1860. The filament was a strip of carbonised cotton which was placed in a vacuum sealed in a glass bulb so that it wouldn't burn - because carbon (or any other element) won't burn without air or oxygen to burn in. It was hard to produce a good vacuum at the time so the light was not very useful because the filament didn't last long enough. But Swan improved on his design and by 1878 both he and, separately, the American inventor Thomas Alva Edison had produced good workable light bulbs. Edison's bulb was largely the same as Swan's design but with improvements.

Swan demonstrated his new bulb in 1879 and by 1881 the House of Commons was lit by Swan bulbs. In 1883 Eddison and Swan joined forces to form the Eddison and Swan United Electric Light Company. The electric light was on its way.

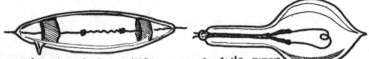

EARLY EXPERIMENTAL ELECTRIC LIGHT BULB

SWAN'S FIRST COMMERCIAL LIGHT BULB

Tennyson, Lord Alfred

poet who took to port

1809-92

Alfred Tennyson was the top poet of the Victorian age, becoming Poet Laureate* to **Queen Victoria** on the death of William Wordsworth in 1850. Prince Albert had loved his poem *In Memoriam*, written for Arthur Hallam, a close friend of Tennyson who died in 1833.

111

I'M STUCK! WHAT RHYMES WITH SHALOTT? CAMELOT, LANCELOT.... ER... ER...

Along with **William Morris** and the **Pre-Raphaelites**, Tennyson shared in the high-Victorian interest in all things medieval. Some of his most famous poems such as *The Lady of Shalott* are on medieval themes. In later life he took to port and tobacco and became self-important, and he was not above the odd stuffy, patriotic poem such as *Britons, guard your own*, written as a warning against the French. But all in all he's well worth reading - even if the old fashioned style creates a slight smell of mothballs in the nose of the reader.

theatre *see* **music halls**

Thomson, Joseph John
discoverer of electrons

1856-1940

For most of the nineteenth century it was widely believed that atoms were the smallest possible things. The word 'atom' comes from the Greek *atomon*, meaning 'indivisible'. Joseph Thomson proved that atoms were divisible after all. By careful experiment at his laboratory in Cambridge he showed that cathode rays, the rays which appear when an electric current passes through a near vacuum, are made up of very tiny particles - very tiny indeed. He proved that these particles, which he called 'corpuscles', were about 2,000 times smaller in mass than atoms of hydrogen, the smallest of all atoms. He made this discovery towards the end of the Victorian period in 1897.

Thomson's particles soon became known as 'electrons'. They were the very first sub-atomic particles to be discovered and led to a revolution in scientific thinking about the atom. Thomson is buried near to Sir Isaac Newton under the nave of Westminster Abbey.

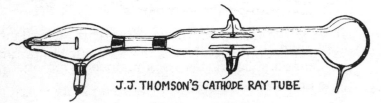

J.J. THOMSON'S CATHODE RAY TUBE

Thomson, William
(Baron Kelvin of Largs)
scientist who dreamed up a scale

1824-1907

William Thomson was a brilliant Scottish scientist and mathematician. He helped to prove that what we call heat is really the movement energy of molecules. When there's no movement - there's no heat. On the Celsius scale, absolute cold happens at minus 273.15°. Thomson invented a temperature scale where absolute zero is 0° but each degree has the same value as a degree Celsius - so there are still 100° between the freezing and boiling points of water. Since on his scale, absolute cold is 0°K, freezing point becomes 273.15° K and boiling point becomes 373.15° K. His scale is called the 'Kelvin Scale' because in 1892 he was made Baron Kelvin.

There are no minus degrees on the Kelvin scale.

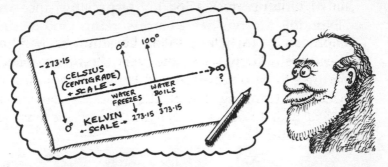

In 1856, Thomson became a director of the Atlantic Telegraph Company. It was his scientific brain more than anything else which made possible the successful completion of a permanent transatlantic telegraph link in 1866. He ended his life a wealthy man and built himself a mock-baronial hall near Largs in Scotland.

Tolpuddle Martyrs
Dorset workers who defied the law
1834

108 **Trades Unions** have never been very popular with employers. Nobody likes to be ganged up on, especially if the purpose of the ganging up is to ask for higher wages. But before 1871, trades unions weren't just unpopular, they were illegal and wages were pitifully low.

Workers who tried to organise themselves into illegal unions were subject to the full wrath of the law. In March 1834 a group of six agricultural labourers from Tolpuddle in Dorset were sentenced to seven years transportation to Australia for recruiting members to the 'Friendly Society of Agricultural Labourers'. The harsh sentence was shocking, especially since the 'Tolpuddle Martyrs' were hard-working, God-fearing men - two of them were Methodist* ministers. They were pardoned two years later in response to public outrage.

Tories *see* **political parties**

trades unions
one for all - almost

Early trades unions were for skilled workers only. Each trade tended to have its own union. In the steel industry for instance, boiler-makers were separate from plate-makers and so on. The Trades Union Congress, founded in 1868 was at first made up of such small unions for skilled men. After trades unions were made legal in the Trade Union Act of 1871, the idea of mass-membership, 'general' unions of the unskilled gradually took hold.

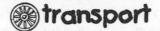

transport

trains, trams and other things on wheels

Railways were by far the most important invention of the nineteenth century. It's hard for us now to imagine how slowly things moved before they were invented. Canals were the main way of shifting freight and horse-drawn carriages were the main way of moving people.

The first railway intended for fare-paying passengers opened in 1830. That was the Manchester-Liverpool line, built by **George Stephenson**. From then on, the construction of paved roads almost stopped for sixty years. Pamphlets were written bemoaning the death of the road system. Likewise canals were abandoned. By 1870 Britain had 13,500 miles of track. Worldwide, total track rose from 5,500 miles in 1840 (mainly in Britain and America) to 466,000 miles in 1900.

HORSE-DRAWN
TRAM, 1883

In towns the biggest advance in transport was the tram - basically train technology put to use on the roads. (Cars were invented in the 1880s but they were far too expensive for most people.) The first tramlines in Britain were laid in Birkenhead and London in 1860 by an American called, appropriately enough, G.F. Train. They were horse drawn.

Roads were improved once more late in the century - mainly because of bicycles. The big breakthrough in bicycle design came in 1874 when the bicycle chain was invented. (Pneumatic tyres followed in 1888.) Mass produced bikes were soon bought in their thousands by the lower classes. Bikes gave a freedom of movement which had been beyond their wildest dreams before.

WHOOPEEE! BICYCLE, 1885

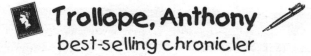

Trollope, Anthony
best-selling chronicler

1815-82

In 1841 Anthony Trollope was made Post-Office Surveyor of Ireland (then a part of the United Kingdom) and in the 1850s, he became Inspector of Deliveries in Ireland. He spent a large chunk of his life travelling the highways and byways of Ireland, meeting all manner of people. He was a friendly sort of man with a rough, cheerful way of speaking. Among other things he is said to have introduced post boxes to Britain.

However, he's most famous for his novels. He started writing in 1843. For years he got up every morning at 5.30 and wrote exactly 2,500 words before breakfast. He's best known for his humorous chronicles (novels) of church life in the fictional town of Barchester in the fictional county of Barsetshire.

HAH! 'OBADIAH SLOPE'! WHAT A GREAT NAME! YOU'RE A GENIUS, TROLLOPE OLD CHAP!

👑 Victoria, Queen
little, fat woman in black

1819-1901

Victoria was just eighteen when she became Queen of Great Britain. She was under five feet tall with fair hair and she liked dancing. It's amazing that she became queen at all since her two drunken uncles, Kings George IV and William IV, had thirteen children between them, but the whole lot died young or were illegitimate* so they couldn't inherit the throne. Victoria was a Hanoverian, a German dynasty, and her first language was German. She learned English when she was three. She ruled for sixty-four years, almost the entire time that Britain was world super-power.

To start with, Victoria adored her first Prime Minister, Lord Melbourne, to the extent that people shouted 'Mrs Melbourne' at her in the street. But then she fell in love with her future husband, **Prince Albert**. They were happily married for twenty-one years and had nine children together. After Albert died in 1861, Victoria hid herself away and wore nothing but black for years and years. Among her closest companions were a Scottish servant called John Brown and, later, an Indian servant called 'the Munshi'. She became known as the 'royal malingerer' because she failed to carry out any royal engagements.

It wasn't until 1876 that she began to come out of
41 hiding, when Prime Minister **Disraeli** arranged for her to become Empress of India (then part of the
17 **British Empire**). By the time of the Golden Jubilee of her reign in 1887, she was more popular than she'd ever been. Millions from all over the world celebrated with her.

voting
how it spread

The British Parliament is known as the 'mother of parliaments' and in many ways it is. It dates back to the Middle Ages. It's so old and so respected that people often see no need to change it. The French had their revolution in 1789 and universal male suffrage* by 1848. The German imperial parliament had universal male suffrage by 1871 (not that that made Germany very democratic). The British mother of parliaments changed more slowly.

By the early nineteenth century, huge new industrial cities such as Manchester and Birmingham had sprung up. They had no MPs to represent them. Meanwhile tiny country 'rotten boroughs' and 'pocket boroughs' elected MPs who were 'in the pockets' of the local aristocracy. The first Reform Bill (1832) slashed the number of rotten and pocket boroughs and gave more MPs to the big cities. It also increased the number of men who were allowed to vote by 57% to 217,000, thus including many of the newly-rich middle class in the electorate*.

17   In 1867 **Disraeli** increased the number of men allowed to vote still further, to 938,000, so that many working class men in the big industrial towns were able to vote for the first time. Further reform acts in 1884-5 gave the vote to male agricultural workers as well.

Campaigns for women to be allowed to vote started in the 1860s. Women over the age of thirty won the right to vote in 1918. By the late 1920s nearly all adults over the age of twenty-one could vote.

Webb, Matthew
swimmer of the Channel
1848-83

Matthew Webb from Dawley in Shropshire was incredibly tough. At twenty-five he won a bet by staying in the water for 1.5 hours longer than a Newfoundland dog - the poor dog nearly drowned.

On 24 August 1875, he smeared his body in porpoise grease to stop him from becoming waterlogged and at 1.00 in the afternoon, having made one unsuccessful attempt a few days earlier, he dived into the sea from the Admiralty Pier at Dover thus starting his epic swim across the English Channel to France. Swimming for almost twenty-two hours continuously through a moonlit night, he reached Calais at 10.40 the next morning. He had been fed cod liver oil, beef tea, brandy, coffee and strong beer from a launch but had not been supported in any other way. Thus he became the first person ever to swim the Channel.

On 24 July 1883, he tried to swim across the turbulent water beneath the Niagara Falls on the border between the USA and Canada. He drowned within eight minutes.

Wilde, Oscar O'Flahertie Wills
clever playwright who went to prison

1856-1900

Oscar Wilde was the cleverest and funniest of all Victorian playwrights. When young he became the leader of a group of Oxford students who called themselves the 'aesthetes'. They wore longish hair and velvet breeches. Wilde pretended to take nothing seriously and to be extremely lazy (although he wasn't really). His motto was 'art for art's sake' which is why he once said that he hoped to 'live up to his blue china'.

Most famous of his plays are: *Lady Windermere's Fan* (1892), *A Woman of no Importance* (1893), *An Ideal Husband* (1895) and *The Importance of being Earnest: a trivial comedy for serious people* (1895). They're almost as funny today as when they were first staged.

In 1895, after a scandal over his close relationship with Alfred Douglas, the son of the Marquis of Queensberry, he was sentenced to two years' hard labour. He career was ruined and he was made bankrupt - Victorian society couldn't cope with someone as outrageous as Oscar. After he came out of prison, he lived mainly in Paris under the name 'Sebastian Melmoth', and it was there in 1898 that he wrote his last great work, *The Ballad of Reading Jail*, about the experience of being a prisoner. His last words are said to have been: 'Either this wallpaper goes or I do'. It's the sort of thing he might have said, although probably someone made it up later.

'...YET EACH MAN KILLS THE THING HE LOVES... THE COWARD DOES IT WITH A KISS, THE BRAVE MAN WITH A SWORD...' GOOD LORD, OSCAR— IT'S FAR TOO SERIOUS!

women
half the nation

56 The **Industrial Revolution** affected women as much as men. Before it got under way, most work had centred round the home or near to it. Very often all the family worked together. But factories were different. There was (and is) very little connection between life at home and life in a factory. Of course women as well as men worked in the factories, but 42 well-meaning legislation such as the **Factories Acts** reduced the hours they could work and the jobs they could do.

More than ever, men became the main earners. As a result men gained power and women lost it. That was partly why during the Victorian age, ideas about the differences between the sexes were very extreme. You can see this in their clothes. The women wore big, impractical but colourful skirts and dresses. The men wore dark, relatively simple trousers and jackets. At best, women were frail, feeble butterflies to be looked after, at worst they were drudges to be bossed about. Clever women who were rich, with **92** **servants** so that they didn't have to do housework, often became so bored that they had the 'vapours'. Fainting was a fashionable female occupation, as was 'hysteria' which amounted to much the same thing.

It couldn't last. More and more women were being educated. In 1865, the first Women's Suffrage* Committee was formed in Manchester to demand women's right to vote. By the 1870s a petition of more than three million signatures had been delivered to Parliament. The fact that women didn't get the vote in Victorian times (except in local elections and then only if they were tax payers) was **111** partly due to **Victoria** herself. She was bitterly opposed to women voting and the two great Prime **41** Ministers of the age, **Disraeli** and **Gladstone**, were **49** worried about offending her.

workhouses
where poor people got put

Under the Poor Law of 1601 each English parish* had to pay for the upkeep of its very poorest members. Often they were housed in 'workhouses' and forced to work in the hope that the parish would save money from their labour. Since the very poor tended to be the sick, the very old or the very young, workhouses never made much money but that wasn't the point somehow.

If anything, workhouses got worse in the Victorian period. The Poor Law Amendment Act of 1834 set out to standardise things and to discourage very poor people from scrounging. They weren't allowed to receive help at home, even if they had a home - they had to go and live in the workhouse if they wanted any sort of help at all. Once in the workhouse, sexes were separated so that families were split up, uniforms were dreary, rules were harsh and the work was very, very long and boring. Conditions improved a little towards the end of the century but fear of the workhouse was a nightmare which haunted every working class family in the nineteenth century.

Zulu War
the British Empire in action
1879

In the 1820s the newly-forged Zulu nation rampaged through Natal in southern Africa in a campaign known as the *Mfecane*, the 'Crushing'. Two million Africans died in the havoc. The Zulus had been organised into a fearsome military machine by their king Shaka, a ruthless dictator who demanded total obedience. You can get a hint of his personality from the name of his capital: *kwaBulawayo* - 'At the Place of He Who Kills - with Afflictions'. He divided his men into regiments, or *impi*, based on age groups. Their weapon was the short stabbing spear, the *iKlwa*, so called from the sucking sound it made when withdrawn from a victim's body. They were superb warriors. They could travel fifty miles in a day, trotting on bare feet, and then fight a battle. Their standard tactic was to pin down the enemy in the centre while the horns of their army raced out to encircle him and attack from behind.

ZULU WARRIOR

By the 1870s Shaka was long gone and a dynamic, new king, Cetshwayo, was in charge. Cetshwayo was a threat to expanding British power in the region and they were a threat to him. In January 1879, with only the feeblest of excuses, the British invaded. They were soundly defeated at the Battle of Isandhlwana (January 1879) when a Zulu army of 20,000 overwhelmed the British force - even though the British had guns and the Zulus didn't. The British lost 1,200 men. The Zulu impis then besieged the British base at the small settlement of Rorke's Drift, but the 120 defenders were ready for them. With the aid of their modern weapons, these 120 held off the entire Zulu army in one of the great heroic feats of the Victorian period.

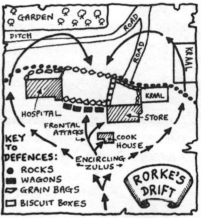

The Zulus were of course defeated - *iKlwas* are no match for guns. Cetshwayo's capital of Ulundi was taken in July and burned to the ground. But the Zulus retained their land, which is now a part of South Africa.

ELEVEN VICTORIA CROSSES WERE AWARDED 'FOR VALOUR' AT RORKE'S DRIFT AND ISANDHLWANA

GLOSSARY

CATHOLICS: Members of the Roman Catholic Church. The Pope based in Rome is their leader.

CONSCRIPTION: Compulsory enlistment in the armed forces.

ELECTORATE: The group of people who are allowed to vote for a government or other democratic institution.

EMANCIPATE: To grant freedom from slavery or some other restriction. It has also come to mean the granting of the right to vote.

EMULSION: A mixture of two liquids, one being spread out in the other in the form of tiny droplets.

ILLEGITIMATE: The children of unmarried parents were said to be illegitimate, meaning not lawful. They did not inherit equally with legitimate brothers and sisters when the parents died - or did not inherit at all.

IMPORT DUTY: Taxes paid on goods brought into a country.

LIBERAL PARTY: Political party which grew out of the old, aristocratic Whig party in Victorian times. Liberals had varying beliefs but all agreed that society progresses best if individuals are *free* - as much as that is possible. The name comes from the Latin word *liber* which means 'free'.

MANIFESTO: The wish-list of a government, political party, or movement. Their manifesto sets out what they hope to achieve.

METHODISTS: The Methodist Church is an offshoot of the Church of England. It was started in the eighteenth century by the brothers John and Charles Wesley.

PARISHES: A parish is the basic administrative area of the church and, until recently, of local government too - as it still is in country areas. A parish has its own church and clergyman. Modern parishes may have several churches and sometimes several clergymen (or women).

PATENTS: Inventors can apply for a patent on their invention. The patent gives them the sole right to make, use or make money from their invention for a set number of years.

POET LAUREATE: The Poet Laureate is paid a small pension by the king or queen in return for writing poems for special state occasions. It's a great honour for the poet who is chosen.

PROTESTANTS: Protestants broke away from the Roman Catholic Church in the early sixteenth century. They were called Protestants because they *protested* about corruption and other practices in the Catholic Church which they thought were unchristian.

QUAKERS: An extreme Protestant group which started in the seventeenth century. Like other 'dissenters' they were barred from the government and the universities. Many of them took to trade instead and some Quaker families became very rich and successful.

SUFFRAGE: The right to vote.

TORIES: Tory was originally a rude name for an Irish Catholic outlaw, a name thrown at supporters of the ousted Catholic King James II in the late 1600s. Later the Tories became firm supporters of the Church of England and in Victorian times they evolved into the modern Conservative Party.

UNITARIANS: The Unitarians evolved from English Presbyterians (a form of Protestantism now widely practised in Scotland). Unitarians became very free thinking towards the end of the eighteenth century. They're called Unitarians because they believe in the unity of God - that he cannot be split into the Trinity of Father, Son and Holy Ghost. In other words, they don't think that Christ is divine.

Index

NOW READ ON

If you want to know more about the Victorians, see if your local library or bookshop has either of these books.

ALL ABOUT THE VICTORIANS
By Jane Goodwin (Hodder Wayland, 2001).
This book is about the most important people and events of the Victorian era. It also looks at changes to work and transport, at the factory system and working life, at the growth of industrial towns and at seaside holidays and entertainment.

WHAT DO WE KNOW ABOUT THE VICTORIANS?
By Richard Tames (Hodder Wayland, 1997).
Using archaeological evidence and excellent artwork, Richard Tames opens an exciting new door on the Victorians. Did Victorians have families like ours? Did they live in houses? Were there Victorian artists? These are just some of the questions he asks - and answers!

ABOUT THE AUTHOR

Bob Fowke is a well-known author of children's information books. Writing under various pen names and with various friends and colleagues, he has created many unusual and entertaining works on all manner of subjects.

There's always more to his books than meets the eye - look at all the entries in the index of this one!

Who? What? When?
ORDER FORM

0 340 85185 6	TUDORS	£4.99
0 340 85184 8	VICTORIANS	£4.99
0 340 85186 4	WORLD WAR I	£4.99
0 340 85187 2	WORLD WAR II	£4.99

All Hodder Children's books are available at your local bookshop or newsagent, or can be ordered direct from the publisher. Just write to the address below. Prices and availability subject to change without notice.

Hodder Children's Books, Cash Sales Department, Bookpoint, 130 Milton Park, Abingdon, Oxon, OX14 4SB, UK.
Email address: orders@bookpoint.co.uk

Please enclose a cheque or postal order made payable to Bookpoint Ltd to the value of the cover price and allow the following for postage and packing:
UK & BFPO - £1.00 for the first book, 50p for the second book, and 30p for each additional book ordered, up to a maximum charge of £3.00. OVERSEAS & EIRE - £2.00 for the first book, £1.00 for the second book, and 50p for each additional book.

If you have a credit card you may order by telephone - (01235) 400414 (lines open 9am-6pm, Monday to Saturday; 24 hour message answering service). Alternatively you can send a fax on 01235 400454.